# 13th Conference of the European Chapter of the Association for Computational Linguistics 2012 (EACL 2012)

# Student Research Workshop



**Avignon, France**
**23 – 27 April 2012**

ISBN: 978-1-62276-501-0

**Printed from e-media with permission by:**

Curran Associates, Inc.
57 Morehouse Lane
Red Hook, NY 12571

CURRAN ASSOCIATES INC.
proceedings.com

**Some format issues inherent in the e-media version may also appear in this print version.**



Printed by Curran Associates, Inc. (2012)



Association for Computational Linguistics
209 N. Eighth Street
Stroudsburg, Pennsylvania 18360

Phone: 1-570-476-8006
Fax: 1-570-476-0860

acl@aclweb.org

**Additional copies of this publication are available from:**

Curran Associates, Inc.
57 Morehouse Lane
Red Hook, NY 12571 USA
Phone: 845-758-0400
Fax: 845-758-2634
Email: curran@proceedings.com
Web: www.proceedings.com

# Introduction

On behalf of the Programme Committee, we are pleased to present the proceedings of the Student Research Workshop held at the 13th Conference of the European Chapter of the Association for Computational Linguistics, in Avignon, France, on April 26, 2012. Following the tradition of providing a forum for student researchers and the success of the previous workshops held in Bergen (1999), Toulouse (2001), Budapest (2003), Trento (2006) and Athens (2009), a panel of senior researchers will take part in the presentation of the papers, providing detailed comments on the work of the authors.

The Student Workshop will run as three parallel sessions, during which 10 papers will be presented. These high standard papers were carefully chosen from a total of 38 submissions coming from 20 countries, and one of them will be awarded the EACL-2012 Best Student Paper.

We would like to take this opportunity to thank the many people that have contributed in various ways to the success of the Student Workshop: the members of the Programme Committee for their evaluation of the submissions and for taking the time to provide useful detailed comments and suggestions for the improvement of papers; the nine panelists for providing detailed feedback on-site; and the students for their hard work in preparing their submissions.

We are also very grateful to the EACL for providing sponsorship for students who would otherwise be unable to attend the workshop and present their work. And finally, thanks to those who have given us advice and assistance in planning this workshop (especially Laurence Danlos, Tania Jimenez, Lluís Màrquez, Mirella Lapata and Walter Daelemans).

We hope you enjoy the Student Research Workshop.

Pierre Lison, University of Oslo
Mattias Nilsson, Uppsala University
Marta Recasens, Stanford University

EACL 2012 Student Research Workshop Co-Chairs

**Program Chairs:**

Pierre Lison, University of Oslo (Norway)
Mattias Nilsson, Uppsala University (Sweden)
Marta Recasens, Stanford University (USA)

**Faculty Advisor:**

Laurence Danlos, University Paris 7 (France)

**Program Committee:**

Lars Ahrenberg, Linköping University (Sweden)
Gemma Boleda, Universitat Politècnica de Catalunya (Spain)
Johan Bos, Rijksuniversiteit Groningen (Netherlands)
Claire Cardie, Cornell University (USA)
Michael Carl, Copenhagen Business School (Denmark)
Benoit Crabbé, University of Paris 7 (France)
Laurence Danlos, University of Paris 7 (France)
Koenraad de Smedt, University of Bergen (Norway)
Micha Elsner, Edinburgh University (UK)
Cédrick Fairon, University of Louvain (Belgium)
Caroline Gasperin, TouchType Ltd (UK)
Nizar Habash, Columbia University (USA)
Barry Haddow, University of Edinburgh (UK)
Laura Hasler, University of Strathclyde (UK)
Graeme Hirst, University of Toronto (Canada)
Jerry Hobbs, University of Southern California (USA)
Véronique Hoste, University College Gent (Belgium)
Sophia Katrenko, Utrecht University (Netherlands)
Jun'ichi Kazama, NICT (Japan)
Dietrich Klakow, University of Saarland (Germany)
Valia Kordoni, University of Saarland (Germany)
Zornitsa Kozareva, University of Southern California (USA)
Marco Kuhlmann, Uppsala University (Sweden)
Sobha Lalitha Devi, AU-KBC Research Centre (India)
Jan Tore Lønning, University of Oslo (Norway)
M. Antònia Martí, University of Barcelona (Spain)
Haitao Mi, Chinese Academy of Sciences (China)
Marie-Francine Moens, K.U.Leuven (Belgium)
Roser Morante, University of Antwerp (Belgium)
Alessandro Moschitti, University of Trento (Italy)
Costanza Navarretta, University of Copenhagen (Denmark)
John Nerbonne, Rijksuniversiteit Groningen (Netherlands)
Constantin Orasan, University of Wolverhampton (UK)
Lilja Øvrelid, University of Oslo (Norway)
Gerald Penn, University of Toronto (Canada)
Adam Przepiórkowski, University of Warsaw (Poland)
Sujith Ravi, Yahoo Research (USA)
Jonathon Read, University of Oslo (Norway)
Horacio Rodríguez, Universitat Politècnica de Catalunya (Spain)

Dan Roth, University of Illinois at Urbana-Champaign (USA)
Marta Ruiz Costa-jussà, Barcelona Media Research Center (Spain)
David Schlangen, Bielefeld University (Germany)
Anders Søgaard, University of Copenhagen (Denmark)
Lucia Specia, University of Wolverhampton (UK)
Caroline Sporleder, University of Saarland (Germany)
Manfred Stede, University of Potsdam (Germany)
Mariona Taulé, University of Barcelona (Spain)
Stefan Thater, University of Saarland (Germany)
Antal van den Bosch, Tilburg University (Netherlands)
Erik Velldal, University of Oslo (Norway)

**Panelists:**

Marco Baroni, University of Trento (Italy)
Myroslava Dzikovska, University of Edinburgh (UK)
Judith Eckle-Kohler, University of Stuttgart (Germany)
Micha Elsner, University of Edinburgh (UK)
Jesús Giménez, Google (Ireland)
Graeme Hirst, University of Toronto (Canada)
Ivan Titov, Saarland University (Germany)
Marco Turchi, Joint Research Centre – IPSC (Italy)
Kalliopi Zervanou, Tilburg University (Netherlands)

# Table of Contents

# Conference Program

*Improving Pronoun Translation for Statistical Machine Translation*
Liane Guillou

*Cross-Lingual Genre Classification*
Philipp Petrenz

*A Comparative Study of Reinforcement Learning Techniques on Dialogue Management*
Alexandros Papangelis

*Manually constructed context-free grammar for Myanmar syllable structure*
Tin Htay Hlaing

*What's in a Name? Entity Type Variation across Two Biomedical Subdomains*
Claudiu Mihăilă and Riza Theresa Batista-Navarro

*Yet Another Language Identifier*
Martin Majliš

*Discourse Type Clustering using POS n-gram Profiles and High-Dimensional Embeddings*
Christelle Cocco

*Hierarchical Bayesian Language Modelling for the Linguistically Informed*
Jan A. Botha

*Mining Co-Occurrence Matrices for SO-PMI Paradigm Word Candidates*
Aleksander Wawer

*Improving machine translation of null subjects in Italian and Spanish*
Lorenza Russo, Sharid Loáiciga and Asheesh Gulati

# Improving Pronoun Translation for Statistical Machine Translation

**Liane Guillou**
School of Informatics
University of Edinburgh
Edinburgh, UK, EH8 9AB
L.K.Guillou@sms.ed.ac.uk

## Abstract

Machine Translation is a well–established field, yet the majority of current systems translate sentences in isolation, losing valuable contextual information from previously translated sentences in the discourse. One important type of contextual information concerns who or what a coreferring pronoun corefers to (i.e., its *antecedent*). Languages differ significantly in how they achieve coreference, and awareness of antecedents is important in choosing the correct pronoun. Disregarding a pronoun's antecedent in translation can lead to inappropriate coreferring forms in the target text, seriously degrading a reader's ability to understand it.

This work assesses the extent to which *source-language annotation* of coreferring pronouns can improve English–Czech Statistical Machine Translation (SMT). As with previous attempts that use this method, the results show little improvement. This paper attempts to explain why and to provide insight into the factors affecting performance.

## 1 Introduction

It is well-known that in many natural languages, a pronoun that corefers must bear similar features to its antecedent. These can include similar number, gender (morphological or referential), and/or animacy. If a pronoun and its antecedent occur in the same unit of translation (N-gram or syntactic tree), these agreement features can influence the translation. But this locality cannot be guaranteed in either phrase-based or syntax-based Statistical Machine Translation (SMT). If it is not within the same unit, a coreferring pronoun will be translated without knowledge of its antecedent, meaning that its translation will simply reflect local frequency. Incorrectly translating a pronoun can result in readers/listeners identifying the wrong antecedent, which can mislead or confuse them.

There have been two recent attempts to solve this problem within the framework of phrase-based SMT (Hardmeier & Federico, 2010; Le Nagard & Koehn, 2010). Both involve *annotation projection*, which in this context means annotating coreferential pronouns in the source-language with features derived from the translation of their aligned antecedents, and then building a *translation model* of the annotated forms. When translating a coreferring pronoun in a new source-language text, the antecedent is identified and its translation used (differently in the two attempts cited above) to annotate the pronoun prior to translation.

The aim of this work was to better understand why neither of the previous attempts achieved more than a small improvement in translation quality associated with coreferring pronouns. Only by understanding this will it be possible to ascertain whether the method of *annotation projection* is intrinsically flawed or the unexpectedly small improvement is due to other factors.

Errors can arise when:

1. Deciding whether or not a third person pronoun corefers;
2. Identifying the pronoun antecedent;
3. Identifying the head of the antecedent, which serves as the source of its features;
4. Aligning the source and target texts at the phrase and word levels.

Factoring out the first two decisions would show whether the lack of significant improvement was simply due to imperfect coreference resolution. In order to control for these errors several different manually annotated versions of the Penn *Wall Street Journal* corpus were used, each providing different annotations over the same text. The BBN Pronoun Coreference and Entity Type corpus (Weischedel & Brunstein, 2005) was used to provide coreference information in the source-language and exclude non-referential pronouns. It also formed the source-language side of the parallel training corpus. The PCEDT 2.0 corpus (Hajič et al., 2011), which contains a close Czech translation of the Penn *Wall Street Journal* corpus, provided reference translations for testing and the target-language side of the parallel corpus for training. To minimise (although not completely eliminate) errors associated with antecedent head identification (item 3 above), the parse trees in the Penn Treebank 3.0 corpus (Marcus et al., 1999) were used. The *gold standard* annotation provided by these corpora allowed me to assume perfect identification of coreferring pronouns and coreference resolution and near–perfect antecedent head noun identification. These assumptions could not be made if state-of-the-art methods had been used as they cannot yet achieve sufficiently high levels of accuracy.

The remainder of the paper is structured as follows. The use of pronominal coreference in English and Czech and the problem of anaphora resolution are described in Section 2. The works of Le Nagard & Koehn (2010) and Hardmeier & Federico (2010) are discussed in Section 3, and the source-language annotation projection method is described in Section 4. The results are presented and discussed in Section 5 and future work is outlined in Section 6.

## 2 Background

### 2.1 Anaphora Resolution

Anaphora resolution involves identifying the antecedent of a referring expression, typically a pronoun or noun phrase that is used to refer to something previously mentioned in the discourse (its antecedent). Where multiple referring expressions refer to the same antecedent, they are said to be *coreferential*. Anaphora resolution and the related task of coreference resolution have been the subject of considerable research within Natural Language Processing (NLP). Excellent surveys are provided by Strube (2007) and Ng (2010).

Unresolved anaphora can add significant translation ambiguity, and their incorrect translation can significantly decrease a reader's ability to understand a text. Accurate coreference in translation is therefore necessary in order to produce understandable and cohesive texts. This justifies recent interest (Le Nagard & Koehn, 2010; Hardmeier & Federico, 2010) and motivates the work presented in this paper.

### 2.2 Pronominal Coreference in English

Whilst English makes some use of case, it lacks the grammatical gender found in other languages. For monolingual speakers, the relatively few different pronoun forms in English make sentences easy to generate: Pronoun choice depends on the number and gender of the entity to which they refer. For example, when talking about ownership of a book, English uses the pronouns "his/her" to refer to a book that belongs to a male/female owner, and "their" to refer to one with multiple owners (irrespective of their gender). One source of difficulty is that the pronoun "it" has both a coreferential and a pleonastic function. A pleonastic pronoun is one that is not referential. For example, in the sentence "It is raining", "it" does not corefer with anything. Coreference resolution algorithms must exclude such instances in order to prevent the erroneous identification of an antecedent when one does not exist.

### 2.3 Pronominal Coreference in Czech

Czech, like other Slavic languages, is highly inflective. It is also a free word order language, in which word order reflects the information structure of the sentence within the current discourse. Czech has seven cases and four grammatical genders: masculine animate (for people and animals), masculine inanimate (for inanimate objects), feminine and neuter. (With feminine and neuter genders, animacy is not grammatically marked.) In Czech, a pronoun must agree in number, gender and animacy with its antecedent. The morphological form of possessive pronouns depends not only on the possessor but also the object in possession. Moreover, reflexive pronouns (both personal and possessive) are commonly used. In addition, Czech is a pro-drop language, whereby an explicit subject pronoun may be omitted if it is inferable from other grammatical features such as verb morphology. This is in contrast with English which exhibits relatively fixed Subject-Verb-Object (SVO) order and only drops subject pronouns in imperatives (e.g. "Stop babbling") and coordinated VPs.

Differences between the choice of coreferring expressions used in English and Czech can be seen in the following simple examples:

1. The dog has a ball. I can see **it** playing outside.
2. The cow is in the field. I can see **it** grazing.
3. The car is in the garage. I will take **it** to work.

In each example, the English pronoun "it" refers to an entity that has a different gender in Czech. Its correct translation requires identifying the gender (and number) of its antecedent and ensuring that the pronoun agrees. In 1 "it" refers to the dog ("pes", masculine, animate) and should be translated as "ho". In 2, "it" refers to the cow ("kráva", feminine) and should be translated as "ji". In 3, "it" refers to the car ("auto", neuter) and should be translated as "ho".

In some cases, the same pronoun is used for both animate and inanimate masculine genders, but in general, different pronouns are used. For example, with possessive reflexive pronouns in the accusative case:

**English:** *I admired* ***my (own)*** *dog*
**Czech:** *Obdivoval jsme* ***svého*** *psa*

**English:** *I admired* ***my (own)*** *castle*
**Czech:** *Obdivoval jsme* ***svůj*** *hrad*

Here "svého" is used to refer to a dog (masculine animate, singular) and "svůj" to refer to a castle (masculine inanimate, singular), both of which belong to the speaker.

Because a pronoun may take a large number of morphological forms in Czech and because case is not checked in annotation projection, the method presented here for translating coreferring pronouns does not guarantee their correct form.

## 3 Related Work

Early work on integrating anaphora resolution with Machine Translation includes the rule-based approaches of Mitkov et al. (1995) and Lappin & Leass (1994) and the transfer-based approach of Saggion & Carvalho (1994). Work in the 1990's culminated in the publication of a special issue of *Machine Translation* on anaphora resolution (Mitkov, 1999). Work then appears to have been on hold until papers were published by Le Nagard & Koehn (2010) and Hardmeier & Federico (2010). This resurgence of interest follows advances since the 1990's which have made new approaches possible.

The work described in this paper resembles that of Le Nagard & Koehn (2010), with two main differences. The first is the use of manually annotated corpora to extract coreference information and morphological properties of the target translations of the antecedents. The second lies in the choice of language pair. They consider English-French translation, focussing on gender-correct translation of the third person pronouns "it" and "they". Coreference is more complex in Czech with both number and gender influencing pronoun selection. Annotating pronouns with both number and gender further exacerbates the problem of data sparseness in the training data, but this cannot be avoided if the aim is to improve their translation. This work also accommodates a wider range of English pronouns.

In contrast, Hardmeier & Federico (2010) focus on English-German translation and model coreference using a word dependency module integrated within the log-linear SMT model as an additional feature function.

Annotation projection has been used elsewhere in SMT. Gimpel & Smith (2008) use it to capture long–distance phenomena within a single sentence in the source-language text via the extraction of sentence-level contextual features, which are used to augment SMT translation models and better predict phrase translation. Projection techniques have also been applied to multilingual Word Sense Disambiguation whereby the sense of a word may be determined in another language (Diab, 2004; Khapra et al., 2009).

## 4 Methodology

### 4.1 Overview

I have followed Le Nagard & Koehn (2010) in using a two-step approach to translation, with *annotation projection* incorporated as a pre-processing

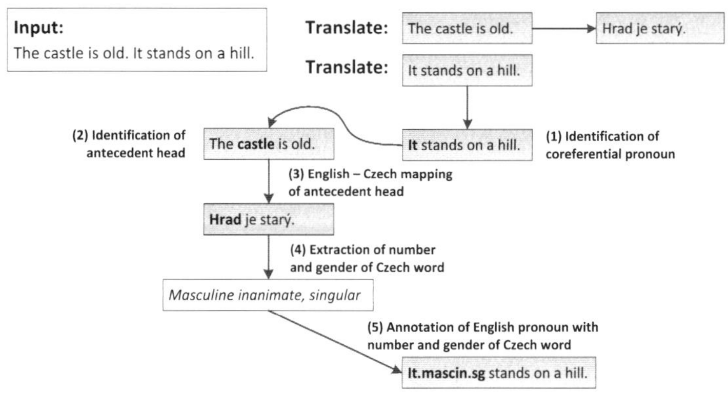


Figure 1: Overview of the Annotation Process

task. In the first step, pronouns are annotated in the source-language text before the text is translated by a phrase-based SMT system in the second step. This approach leaves the translation process unaffected. In this work, the following pronouns are annotated: third person personal pronouns (except instances of "it" that are pleonastic or that corefer with clauses or VPs), reflexive personal pronouns and possessive pronouns, including reflexive possessives. Relative pronouns are excluded as they are local dependencies in both English and Czech and this work is concerned with the longer range dependencies typically exhibited by the previously listed pronoun types.

Annotation of the English source-language text and its subsequent translation into Czech is achieved using two phrase-based translation systems. The first, hereafter called the *Baseline system*, is trained using English and Czech sentence–aligned parallel training data with no annotation. The second system, hereafter called the *Annotated system*, is trained using the same target data, but in the source-language text, each coreferring pronoun has been annotated with number, gender and animacy features. These are obtained from the existing (Czech reference) translation of the head of its English antecedent. Word alignment of English and Czech is obtained from the PCEDT 2.0 alignment file which maps English words to their corresponding t-Layer (deep syntactic, tectogrammatical) node in the Czech translation. Starting with this t-Layer node the annotation layers of the PCEDT 2.0 corpus are traversed and the number and gender of the Czech word are extracted from the morphological layer (m-Layer).

The Baseline system serves a dual purpose. It forms the first stage of the two-step translation process, and as described in Section 5, it provides a baseline against which Annotated system translations are compared.

The annotation process used here is shown in Figure 1. It identifies coreferential pronouns and their antecedents using the annotation in the BBN Pronoun Coreference and Entity Type corpus, and obtains the Czech translation of the English antecedent from the translation produced by the Baseline system. Because many antecedents come from previous sentences, these sentences must be translated before translating the current sentence. Here I follow Le Nagard & Koehn (2010) in translating the complete source-language text using the Baseline system and then extracting the (here, Czech) translations of the English antecedents from the output. This provides a simple solution to the problem of obtaining the Czech translation prior to annotation. In contrast Hardmeier & Federico (2010) translate sentence by sentence using a process which was deemed to be more complex than was necessary for this project.

The English text is annotated such that all coreferential pronouns whose antecedents have an identifiable Czech translation are marked with the number and gender of that Czech word. The output of the annotation process is thus the same English text that was input to the Baseline system, with the addition of annotation of the coreferential pronouns. This annotated English text is then translated using the Annotated translation system, the output of which is the final translation.

| | Training | Dev. | Final |
|---|---|---|---|
| Parallel Sentences | 47,549 | 280 | 540 |
| Czech Words | 955,018 | 5,467 | 10,110 |
| English Words | 1,024,438 | 6,114 | 11,907 |

Table 1: Sizes of the training and testing datasets

### 4.2 Baseline and Annotated systems

Both systems are phrase-based SMT models, trained using the Moses toolkit (Hoang et al., 2007). They share the same 3-gram language model constructed from the target-side text of the parallel training corpus and the Czech monolingual 2010 and 2011 News Crawl corpora[1]. The language model was constructed using the SRILM toolkit (Stolcke, 2002) with interpolated Kneser-Ney discounting (Kneser & Ney, 1995). In addition, both systems are forced to use the same word alignments (constructed using Giza++ (Och & Ney, 2003) in both language pair directions and using *stemmed* training data in which words are limited to the first four characters) in order to mitigate the effects of Czech word inflection on word alignment statistics. This helps to ensure that the Czech translation of the head of the antecedent remains constant in both steps of the two-step process. If this were to change it would defeat the purpose of pronoun annotation as different Czech translations could result in different gender and/or number.

The Baseline system was trained using the Penn *Wall Street Journal* corpus with no annotation, while the Annotated system was trained with an annotated version of the same text (see Table 1), with the target-language text being the same in both cases. The Penn *Wall Street Journal* corpus was annotated using the process described above, with the number and gender of the Czech translation of the antecedent head obtained from the PCEDT 2.0 alignment file.

### 4.3 Processing test files

Two test files were used (see Table 1) – one called 'Final' and the other, 'Development' (Dev). A test file is first translated using the Baseline system with a trace added to the Moses decoder. Each coreferential English pronoun is then identified using the BBN Pronoun Coreference and Entity Type corpus and the head of its antecedent is extracted from the annotated NPs in the Penn Treebank 3.0 corpus. The sentence number and word position of the English pronoun and its antecedent head noun(s) are extracted from the input English text and used to identify the English/Czech phrase pairs that contain the Czech translations of the English words. Using this information together with the phrase alignments (output by the Moses decoder) and the phrase-internal word alignments in the phrase translation table, a Czech translation is obtained from the Baseline system. Number, gender and animacy (if masculine) features of the Czech word identified as the translation of the head of the antecedent are extracted from a pre-built morphological dictionary of Czech words constructed from the PCEDT 2.0 corpus for the purpose of this work. A copy of the original English test file is then constructed, with each coreferential pronoun annotated with the extracted Czech features.

The design of this process reflects two assumptions. First, the annotation of the Czech words in the m-Layer of the PCEDT 2.0 corpus is both accurate and consistent. Second, as the Baseline and Annotated systems were trained using the same word alignments, the Czech translation of the head of the English antecedent should be the same in the output of both. Judging by the very small number of cases in which the antecedent translations differed (3 out of 458 instances), this assumption was proved to be reasonable. These differences were due to the use of different phrase tables for each system as a result of training on different data (i.e. the annotation of English pronouns or lack thereof). This would not be an issue for single-step translation systems such as that used by Hardmeier & Federico (2010).

### 4.4 Evaluation

No standard method yet exists for evaluating pronoun translation in SMT. Early work focussed on the development of techniques for anaphora resolution and their integration within Machine Translation (Lappin & Leass, 1994; Saggion & Carvalho, 1994; Mitkov et al., 1995), with little mention of evaluation. In recent work, evaluation has become much more important. Both Le Nagard & Koehn (2010) and Hardmeier & Federico (2010) consider and reject BLEU (Papineni et al., 2002) as ill-suited for evaluating pronoun translation. While Hardmeier & Federico propose and

[1] Provided for the Sixth EMNLP Workshop on Statistical Machine Translation (Callison-Burch et al., 2011)

use a strict recall and precision based metric for English–German translation, I found it unsuitable for English–Czech translation, given the highly inflective nature of Czech.

Given the importance of evaluation to the goal of assessing the effectiveness of *annotation projection* for improving the translation of coreferring pronouns, I carried out two separate types of evaluation — an automated evaluation which could be applied to the entire test set, and an in-depth manual assessment that might provide more information, but could only be performed on a subset of the test set. The automated evaluation is based on the fact that a Czech pronoun must agree in number and gender with its antecedent. Thus one can count the number of pronouns in the translation output for which this agreement holds, rather than simply score the output against a single reference translation. To obtain these figures, the automated evaluation process counted:

1. Total pronouns in the input English test file.
2. Total English pronouns identified as coreferential, as per the annotation of the BBN Pronoun Coreference and Entity Type corpus.
3. Total coreferential English pronouns that are annotated by the annotation process.
4. Total coreferential English pronouns that are aligned with any Czech translation.
5. Total coreferential English pronouns translated as any Czech pronoun.
6. Total coreferential English pronouns translated as a Czech pronoun corresponding to a **valid** translation of the English pronoun.
7. Total coreferential English pronouns translated as a Czech pronoun (that is a valid translation of the English pronoun) agreeing in number and gender with the antecedent.

The representation of valid Czech translations of English pronouns takes the form of a list provided by an expert in Czech NLP, which ignores case and focusses solely on number and gender.

In contrast, the manual evaluation carried out by that same expert, who is also a native speaker of Czech, was used to determine whether deviations from the single reference translation provided in the PCEDT 2.0 corpus were valid alternatives or simply poor translations. The following judgements were provided:

1. Whether the pronoun had been translated correctly, or in the case of a dropped pronoun, whether pro-drop was appropriate;
2. If the pronoun translation was incorrect, whether a native Czech speaker would still be able to derive the meaning;
3. For input to the Annotated system, whether the pronoun had been correctly annotated with respect to the Czech translation of its identified antecedent;
4. Where an English pronoun was translated differently by the Baseline and Annotated systems, which was better. If both translated an English pronoun to a valid Czech translation, equal correctness was assumed.

In order to ensure that the manual assessor was directed to the Czech translations aligned to the English pronouns, additional markup was automatically inserted into the English and Czech texts: (1) coreferential pronouns in both English and Czech texts were marked with the head noun of their antecedent (denoted by *), and (2) coreferential pronouns in the English source texts were marked with the Czech translation of the antecedent head, and those in the Czech target texts were marked with the original English pronoun that they were aligned to:

**English text input to the Baseline system:** *the u.s. , claiming some success in its trade diplomacy , ...*

**Czech translation output by the Baseline system:** *usa , tvrdí někteří její(**its**) obchodní úspěch v diplomacii , ...*

**English text input to the Annotated system:** *the u.s.* , claiming some success in its(**u.s.,usa**).mascin.pl trade diplomacy , ...*

**Czech translation output by the Annotated system:** *usa ,* tvrdí někteří úspěchu ve své(**its.mascin.pl**) obchodní diplomacii , ...*

## 5 Results and Discussion

### 5.1 Automated Evaluation

Automated evaluation of both "Development" and "Final" test sets (see Table 2) shows that even factoring out the problems of accurate identification of coreferring pronouns, coreference resolution and antecedent head–finding, does not improve performance of the Annotated system much above that of the Baseline.

| | Dev. | | Final | |
|---|---|---|---|---|
| | Baseline | Annotated | Baseline | Annotated |
| Total pronouns in English file | 156 | 156 | 350 | 350 |
| Total pronouns identified as coreferential | 141 | 141 | 331 | 331 |
| Annotated coreferential English pronouns | – | 117 | – | 278 |
| Coreferential English pronouns aligned with any Czech translation | 141 | 141 | 317 | 317 |
| Coreferential English pronouns translated as Czech pronouns | 71 | 75 | 198 | 198 |
| Czech pronouns that are valid translations of the English pronouns | 63 | 71 | 182 | 182 |
| Czech pronouns that are valid translations of the English pronouns and that match their antecedent in number and gender | 44 | 46 | 142 | 146 |

Table 2: Automated Evaluation Results for both test sets

| Criterion | Baseline System Better | Annotated System Better | Systems Equal |
|---|---|---|---|
| Overall quality | **9/31** (29.03%) | **11/31** (35.48%) | **11/31** (35.48%) |
| Quality when annotation is correct | **3/18** (16.67%) | **9/18** (50.00%) | **6/18** (33.33%) |

Table 3: Manual Evaluation Results: A direct comparison of pronoun translations that differ between systems

Taking the accuracy of pronoun translation to be the proportion of coreferential English pronouns having a valid Czech translation that agrees in both number and gender with their antecedent, yields the following on the two test sets:

**Baseline system:**

Development — 44/141 (31.21%)

Final — 142/331 (42.90%)

**Annotated system:**

Development — 46/141 (32.62%)

Final — 146/331 (44.10%)

There are, however, several reasons for not taking this evaluation as definitive. Firstly, it relies on the accuracy of the word alignments output by the decoder to identify the Czech translations of the English pronoun and its antecedent. Secondly, these results fail to capture variation between the translations produced by the Baseline and Annotated systems. Whilst there is a fairly high degree of overlap, for approximately 1/3 of the "Development" set pronouns and 1/6 of the "Final" set pronouns, the Czech translation is different. Since the goal of this work was *to understand what is needed in order to improve the translation of coreferential pronouns*, manual evaluation was critical for understanding the potential capabilities of source-side annotation.

## 5.2 Manual Evaluation

The sample files provided for manual evaluation contained 31 pronouns for which the translations provided by the two systems differed (*differences*) and 72 for which the translation provided by the systems was the same (*matches*). Thus, the sample comprised 103 of the 472 coreferential pronouns (about 22%) from across both test sets. Of this sample, it is the *differences* that indicate the relative performance of the two systems. Of the 31 pronouns in this set, 16 were $3^{rd}$-person pronouns, 2 were reflexive personal pronouns and 13 were possessive pronouns.

The results corresponding to evaluation criterion 4 in Section 4.4 provide a comparison of the overall quality of pronoun translation for both systems. These results for the "Development" and "Final" test sets (see Table 3) suggest that the performance of the Annotated system is comparable with, and even marginally better than, that of the Baseline system, especially when the pronoun annotation is correct.

An example of where the Annotated system produces a better translation than the Baseline system is:

**Annotated English:** *he said* ***mexico*** *could be one of the next countries to be removed from the priority list because of* ***its.neut.sg*** *efforts to craft a new patent law .*

**Baseline translation:** *řekl , že* ***mexiko*** *by mohl být jeden z dalších zemí , aby byl odvolán z prioritou seznam , protože* ***její*** *snahy podpořit nové patentový zákon .*

**Annotated translation:** *řekl , že* ***mexiko*** *by mohl být jeden z dalších zemí , aby byl odvolán z prioritou seznam , protože* ***jeho*** *snahy podpořit nové patentový zákon .*

In this example, the English pronoun "its", which refers to "mexico" is annotated as neuter and singular (as extracted from the Baseline translation). Both systems translate "mexico" as "mexiko" (neuter, singular) but differ in their translation of the pronoun. The Baseline system translates "its" incorrectly as "její" (feminine, singular), whereas the Annotated system produces the more correct translation: "jeho" (neuter, singular), which agrees with the antecedent in both number and gender.

An analysis of the judgements on the remaining three evaluation criteria (outlined in Section 4.4) for the 31 *differences* provides further information. The Baseline system appears to be more accurate, with 19 pronouns either correctly translated (in terms of number and gender) or appropriately dropped, compared with 17 for the Annotated system. Of those pronouns, the meaning could still be understood for 7/12 for the Baseline system compared with 8/14 for the Annotated system. On the surface this may seem strange but it appears to be due to a small number of cases in which the translations produced by both systems were incorrect but those produced by the Annotated system were deemed to be marginally better. Due to the small sample size it is difficult to form a complete picture of where one system may perform consistently better than the other. The annotation of both number and gender was accurate for 18 pronouns. Whilst this accuracy is not particularly high, the results (see Table 3) suggest that translation is more accurate for those pronouns that are correctly annotated.

Whilst pro-drop in Czech was not explicitly handled in the annotation process, manual evaluation revealed that both systems were able to successfully 'learn' a few (local) scenarios in which pro-drop is appropriate. This was unexpected but found to be due to instances in which there are short distances between the pronoun and verb in English. For example, many of the occurrences of "she" in English appear in the context of "she said..." and are translated correctly with the verb form "...řekla...".

An example of where the Annotated system correctly drops a pronoun is:

**Annotated English:** *" this is the worst* ***shakeout*** *ever in the junk market , and it could take years before* ***it.fem.sg*** *' s over , " says mark bachmann , a senior vice president at standard & poor ' s corp . , a credit rating company .*

**Baseline translation:** *" je to nejhorší* ***krize*** *, kdy na trhu s rizikovými obligacemi , a to může trvat roky , než je* ***to*** *pryč , " říká mark bachmann , hlavní viceprezident společnosti standard & poor 's corp . , úvěrový rating společnosti .*

**Annotated translation:** *" je to nejhorší* ***krize*** *, kdy na trhu s rizikovými obligacemi , a to může trvat roky , než je !! pryč , " říká mark bachmann , hlavní viceprezident společnosti standard & poor 's corp . , úvěrový rating společnosti .*

In this example, the Baseline system translates "it" incorrectly as the neuter singular pronoun "to", whereas the Annotated system correctly drops the subject pronoun (indicated by !!) — this is a less trivial example than "she said". In the case of the Baseline translation "to" could be interpreted as referring to the whole event, which would be correct, but poor from a stylistic point of view.

An example of where the Annotated system fails to drop a pronoun is:

**Annotated English:** ***taiwan*** *has improved* ***its.mascin.sg**** *standing with the u.s. by initialing a bilateral copyright agreement , amending* ***its.mascin.sg***** *trademark law and introducing legislation to protect foreign movie producers from unauthorized showings of their.mascan.pl films .*

**Annotated translation:** ***tchaj-wan*** *zlepšení* ***své*** *postavení s usa o initialing bilaterálních autorských práv na* ***jeho*** *obchodní dohody , úprava zákona a zavedení zákona na ochranu zahraniční filmové producenty z neoprávněné showings svých filmů .*

**Reference translation**: ***tchaj-wan*** *zlepšil svou reputaci v usa , když podepsal bilaterální smlouvu o autorských právech , pozměnil !! zákon o ochranných známkách a zavedl legislativu na ochranu zahraničních filmových producentů proti neautorizovanému promítání jejich filmů .*

In this example, the English pronoun "its", which refers to "taiwan" is annotated as masculine inanimate and singular. The first occurrence of "its" is marked by * and the second occurrence by ** in the annotated English text above. The second occurrence should be translated either as a reflexive pronoun (as the first occurrence is correctly translated) or it should be dropped as in the reference translation (!! indicates the position of the dropped pronoun).

In addition to the judgements, the manual assessor also provided feedback on the evaluation task. One of the major difficulties encountered concerned the translation of pronouns in sentences which exhibit poor syntactic structure. This is a criticism of Machine Translation as a whole, but of the manual evaluation of pronoun translation in particular, since the choice of coreferring form is sensitive to syntactic structure. Also the effects of poor syntactic structure are likely to introduce an additional element of subjectivity if the assessor must first interpret the structure of the sentences output by the translation systems.

### 5.3 Potential Sources of Error

Related errors that may have contributed to the Annotated system not providing a significant improvement over the Baseline include: (1) incorrect identification of the English antecedent head noun, (2) incorrect identification of the Czech translation of the antecedent head noun in the Baseline output due to errors in the word alignments, and (3) errors in the PCEDT 2.0 alignment file (affecting training only). While "perfect" annotation of the BBN Pronoun Coreference and Entity Type, the PCEDT 2.0 and the Penn Treebank 3.0 corpora has been assumed, errors in these corpora cannot be completely ruled out.

## 6 Conclusion and Future Work

Despite factoring out three major sources of error — identifying coreferential pronouns, finding their antecedents, and identifying the head of each antecedent — through the use of manually annotated corpora, the results of the Annotated system show only a small improvement over the Baseline system. Two possible reasons for this are that the statistics in the phrase translation table have been weakened in the Annotated system as a result of including both number and gender in the annotation and that the size of the training corpus is relatively small.

However, more significant may be the availability of only a single reference translation. This affects the development and application of automated evaluation metrics as a single reference cannot capture the variety of possible valid translations. Coreference can be achieved without explicit pronouns. This is true of both English and Czech, with sentences that contain pronouns having common paraphrases that lack them. For example,

*the u.s. , claiming some success in* ***its*** *trade diplomacy , ...*

can be paraphrased as:

*the u.s. , claiming some success in trade diplomacy , ...*

A target-language translation of the former might actually be a translation of the latter, and hence lack the pronoun shown in bold. Given the range of variability in whether pronouns are used in conveying coreference, the availability of only a single reference translation is a real problem.

Improving the accuracy of coreferential pronoun translation remains an open problem in Machine Translation and as such there is great scope for future work in this area. The investigation reported here suggests that it is not sufficient to focus solely on the source-side and further operations on the target side (besides post-translation application of a target-language model) need also be considered. Other target–side operations could involve the extraction of features to score multiple candidate translations in the selection of the 'best' option – for example, to 'learn' scenarios in which pro-drop is appropriate and to select translations that contain pronouns of the correct morphological inflection. This requires identification of features in the target side, their extraction and incorporation in the translation process which could be difficult to achieve within a purely statistical framework given that the antecedent of a pronoun may be arbitrarily distant in the previous discourse.

The aim of this work was to better understand why previous attempts at using annotation projection in pronoun translation showed less than expected improvement. Thus it would be beneficial to conduct an error analysis to show the frequency of the errors described in Section 5.3 appear.

I will also be exploring other directions related to problems identified during the course of the work completed to date. These include, but are not limited to, handling pronoun dropping in pro-drop languages, developing pronoun-specific automated evaluation metrics and addressing the problem of having only one reference translation for use with such metrics. In this regard, I will be considering the use of paraphrase techniques to generate synthetic reference translations to augment an existing reference translation set. Initial efforts will focus on adapting the approach of Kauchak & Barzilay (2006) and back–translation methods for extracting paraphrases (Bannard & Callison-Burch, 2005) to the more specific problem of pronoun variation.


## Acknowledgements

I would like to thank Bonnie Webber (University of Edinburgh) who supervised this project and Markéta Lopatková (Charles University) who provided the much needed Czech language assistance. I am very grateful to Ondřej Bojar (Charles University) for his numerous helpful suggestions and to the Institute of Formal and Applied Linguistics (Charles University) for providing the PCEDT 2.0 corpus. I would also like to thank Wolodja Wentland and the three anonymous reviewers for their feedback.

## References


Colin Bannard and Chris Callison-Burch. 2005. Paraphrasing with Bilingual Parallel Corpora. In *Proceedings of the 43rd Annual Meeting of the ACL*, pages 597–604.

Chris Callison-Burch, Philipp Koehn, Christof Monz and Omar Zaidan. 2011. Findings of the 2011 Workshop on Statistical Machine Translation. In *Proceedings of the Sixth Workshop on Statistical Machine Translation*, pages 22–64.

Mona Diab. 2004. An Unsupervised Approach for Bootstrapping Arabic Sense Tagging. In *Proceedings of the Workshop on Computational Approaches to Arabic Script-based Languages*, pages 43–50.

Kevin Gimpel and Noah A. Smith. 2008. Rich Source-Side Context for Statistical Machine Translation. In *Proceedings of the Third Workshop on Statistical Machine Translation*, pages 9–17.

Barbara J. Grosz, Scott Weinstein and Aravind K. Joshi. 1995. Centering: A Framework for Modeling the Local Coherence Of Discourse. *Computational Linguistics*, 21(2):203–225.

Christian Hardmeier and Marcello Federico. 2010. Modelling Pronominal Anaphora in Statistical Machine Translation. In *Proceedings of the 7th International Workshop on Spoken Language Translation*, pages 283–290.

Philipp Koehn, Hieu Hoang, Alexandra Birch, Chris Callison-Burch, Marcello Federico, Nicola Bertoldi, Brooke Cowan, Wade Shen, Christine Moran, Richard Zens. Chris Dyer, Ondřej Bojar, Alexandra Constantin and Evan Herbst. 2007. Moses: Open Source Toolkit for Statistical Machine Translation. In *Proceedings of the 45th Annual Meeting of the ACL on Interactive Poster and Demonstration Sessions*, pages 177–180.

Jerry R. Hobbs. 1978. Resolving Pronominal References. *Lingua*, 44:311–338.

Jan Hajič, Eva Hajičová, Jarmila Panevová, Petr Sgall, Silvie Cinková, Eva Fučíková, Marie Mikulová, Petr Pajas, Jan Popelka, Jiří Semecký, Jana Šindlerová, Jan Štěpánek, Josef Toman, Zdeňka Urešová and Zdeněk Žabokrtský. 2011. Prague Czech-English Dependency Treebank 2.0. Institute of Formal and Applied Linguistics. Prague, Czech Republic.

David Kauchak and Regina Barzilay. 2006. Paraphrasing For Automatic Evaluation. In *Proceedings of the Main Conference on Human Language Technology Conference of the NAACL*, June 5–7, New York, USA, pages 455–462.

Mitesh M. Khapra, Sapan Shah, Piyush Kedia and Pushpak Bhattacharyya. 2009. Projecting Parameters for Multilingual Word Sense Disambiguation. In *Proceedings of the 2009 Conference on Empirical Methods in Natural Language Processing*, August 6–7, Singapore, pages 459–467.

Reinhard Kneser and Hermann Ney. 1995. Improved Backing-Off for M-gram Language Modeling. *IEEE International Conference on Acoustics, Speech, and Signal Processing*, May 9–12, Detroit, USA, 1:181–184.

Shalom Lappin and Herbert J. Leass. 1994. An Algorithm for Pronominal Anaphora Resolution. *Computational Linguistics*, 20:535–561.

Ronan Le Nagard and Philipp Koehn. 2010. Aiding Pronoun Translation with Co-reference Resolution. In *Proceedings of the Joint Fifth Workshop on Statistical Machine Translation and MetricsMATR*, pages 252–261.

Vincent Ng. 2010. Supervised Noun Phrase Coreference Research: The first 15 years. In *Proceedings of the 48th Meeting of the ACL*, pages 1396–1411.

Mitchell P. Marcus, Beatrice Santorini, Mary A. Marcinkiewicz and Ann Taylor. 1999. Penn Treebank 3.0 LDC Calalog No.: LDC99T42. Linguistic Data Consortium.

Ruslan Mitkov, Sung-Kwon Choi and Randall Sharp. 1995. Anaphora Resolution in Machine Translation. In *Proceedings of the Sixth International Conference on Theoretical and Methodological Issues in Machine Translation*, July 5-7, Leuven, Belgium, pages 5–7.

Ruslan Mitkov. 1999. Introduction: Special Issue on Anaphora Resolution in Machine Translation and Multilingual NLP. *Machine Translation*, 14:159–161.

Franz J. Och and Hermann Ney. 2003. A Systematic Comparison of Various Statistical Alignment Models. *Computational Linguistics*, 29(1):19–51.

Kishore Papineni, Salim Roukos, Todd Ward and Wei-Jing Zhu. 2002. BLEU: a method for automatic evaluation of machine translation. In *Proceedings of the 40th Annual Meeting of the ACL*, pages 311–318.

Horacio Saggion and Ariadne Carvalho. 1994. Anaphora Resolution in a Machine Translation System. In *Proceedings of the International Conference on Machine Translation: Ten Years On*, November, Cranfield, UK, 4.1-4.14.

Andreas Stolcke. 2002. SRILM — An Extensible Language Modeling Toolkit. In *Proceedings of International Conference on Spoken Language Processing*, September 16-20, Denver, USA, 2:901–904.

Michael Strube. 2007. Corpus-based and Machine Learning Approaches to Anaphora Resolution. *Anaphors in Text: Cognitive, Formal and Applied Approaches to Anaphoric Reference*, John Benjamins Pub Co.

Ralph Weischedel and Ada Brunstein. 2005. BBN Pronoun Coreference and Entity Type Corpus LDC Calalog No.: LDC2005T33. Linguistic Data Consortium.

# Cross-Lingual Genre Classification

**Philipp Petrenz**
School of Informatics, University of Edinburgh
10 Crichton Street, Edinburgh, EH8 9AB, UK
p.petrenz@sms.ed.ac.uk

## Abstract

Classifying text genres across languages can bring the benefits of genre classification to the target language without the costs of manual annotation. This article introduces the first approach to this task, which exploits text features that can be considered *stable genre predictors* across languages. My experiments show this method to perform equally well or better than full text translation combined with monolingual classification, while requiring fewer resources.

## 1 Introduction

Automated text classification has become standard practice with applications in fields such as information retrieval and natural language processing. The most common basis for text classification is by topic (Joachims, 1998; Sebastiani, 2002), but other classification criteria have evolved, including sentiment (Pang et al., 2002), authorship (de Vel et al., 2001; Stamatatos et al., 2000a), and author personality (Oberlander and Nowson, 2006), as well as categories relevant to filter algorithms (e.g., spam or inappropriate contents for minors).

Genre is another text characteristic, often described as orthogonal to topic. It has been shown by Biber (1988) and others after him, that the genre of a text affects its formal properties. It is therefore possible to use cues (e.g., lexical, syntactic, structural) from a text as features to predict its genre, which can then feed into information retrieval applications (Karlgren and Cutting, 1994; Kessler et al., 1997; Finn and Kushmerick, 2006; Freund et al., 2006). This is because users may want documents that serve a particular communicative purpose, as well as being on a particular topic. For example, a web search on the topic "crocodiles" may return an encyclopedia entry, a biological fact sheet, a news report about attacks in Australia, a blog post about a safari experience, a fiction novel set in South Africa, or a poem about wildlife. A user may reject many of these, just because of their genre: Blog posts, poems, novels, or news reports may not contain the kind or quality of information she is seeking. Having classified indexed texts by genre would allow additional selection criteria to reflect this.

Genre classification can also benefit Language Technology indirectly, where differences in the cues that correlate with genre may impact system performance. For example, Petrenz and Webber (2011) found that within the New York Times corpus (Sandhaus, 2008), the word "states" has a higher likelihood of being a verb in letters (approx. 20%) than in editorials (approx. 2%). Part-of-Speech (PoS) taggers or statistical machine translation (MT) systems could benefit from knowing such genre-based domain variation. Kessler et al. (1997) mention that parsing and word-sense disambiguation can also benefit from genre classification. Webber (2009) found that different genres have a different distribution of discourse relations, and Goldstein et al. (2007) showed that knowing the genre of a text can also improve automated summarization algorithms, as genre conventions dictate the location and structure of important information within a document.

All the above work has been done within a single language. Here I describe a new approach to genre classification that is cross-lingual. Cross-lingual genre classification (CLGC) differs from both poly-lingual and language-independent genre classification. CLGC entails training a genre classification model on a set of labeled texts written in a source language $L_S$ and using this model to predict the genres of texts written in the target language $L_T \neq L_S$. In poly-lingual classification, the training set is made up of texts from two or more languages $S = \{L_{S_1}, \ldots, L_{S_N}\}$ that include the target language $L_T \in S$. Language-independent classification approaches are mono-lingual methods that can be applied to any language. Unlike CLGC, both poly-lingual and language-independent genre classification require labeled training data in the target language.

Supervised text classification requires a large amount of labeled data. CLGC attempts to leverage the available annotated data in well-resourced languages like English in order to bring the aforementioned advantages to poorly-resourced languages. This reduces the need for manual annotation of text corpora in the target language. Manual annotation is an expensive and time-consuming task, which, where possible, should be avoided or kept to a minimum. Considering the difficulties researchers are encountering in compiling a genre reference corpus for even a single language (Sharoff et al., 2010), it is clear that it would be infeasible to attempt the same for thousands of other languages.

## 2 Prior work

Work on automated genre classification was first carried out by Karlgren and Cutting (1994). Like Kessler et al. (1997) and Argamon et al. (1998) after them, they exploit (partly) hand-crafted sets of features, which are specific to texts in English. These include counts of function words such as "we" or "therefore", selected PoS tag frequencies, punctuation cues, and other statistics derived from intuition or text analysis. Similarly language specific feature sets were later explored for mono-lingual genre classification experiments in German (Wolters and Kirsten, 1999) and Russian (Braslavski, 2004).

In subsequent research, automatically generated feature sets have become more popular. Most of these tend to be language-independent and might work in mono-lingual genre classification tasks in languages other than English. Examples are the word based approaches suggested by Stamatatos et al. (2000b) and Freund et al. (2006), the image features suggested by Kim and Ross (2008), the PoS histogram frequency approach by Feldman et al. (2009), and the character n-gram approaches proposed by Kanaris and Stamatatos (2007) and Sharoff et al. (2010). All of them were tested exclusively on English texts. While language-independence is a popular argument often claimed by authors, few have shown empirically that this is true of their approach. One of the few authors to carry out genre classification experiments in more than one language was Sharoff (2007). Using PoS 3-grams and a variation of common word 3-grams as feature sets, Sharoff classified English and Russian documents into genre categories. However, while the PoS 3-gram set yielded respectable prediction accuracy for English texts, in Russian documents, no improvement over the baseline of choosing the most frequent genre class was observed.

While there is virtually no prior work on CLGC, cross-lingual methods have been explored for other text classification tasks. The first to report such experiments were Bel et al. (2003), who predicted text topics in Spanish and English documents, using one language for training and the other for testing. Their approach involves training a classifier on language A, using a document representation containing only content words (nouns, adjectives, and verbs with a high corpus frequency). These words are then translated from language B to language A, so that texts in either language are mapped to a common representation.

Thereafter, cross-lingual text classification was typically regarded as a domain adaptation problem that researchers have tried to solve using large sets of unlabeled data and/or small sets of labeled data in the target language. For instance, Rigutini et al. (2005) present an EM algorithm in which labeled source language documents are translated into the target language and then a classifier is trained to predict labels on a large, unlabeled set in the target language. These instances are then used to iteratively retrain the classification model and the predictions are updated until convergence occurs. Using information gain scores at every iteration to only retain the most predictive words and thus reduce noise, Rigutini et al. (2005) achieve a considerable improvement over the baseline accuracy, which is a simple translation of the training instances and subsequent mono-lingual classification. They, too, were classifying texts by topics and used a collection of English and Italian newsgroup messages. Similarly, researchers have used semi-supervised bootstrapping methods like co-training (Wan, 2009) and other domain adaptation methods like structural component learning (Prettenhofer and Stein, 2010) to carry out cross-lingual text classification.

All of the approaches described above rely on MT, even if some try to keep translation to a minimum. This has several disadvantages however, as applications become dependent on parallel corpora, which may not be available for poorly-resourced languages. It also introduces problems due to word ambiguity and morphology, especially where single words are translated out of context. A different method is proposed by Gliozzo and Strapparava (2006), who use latent semantic analysis on a combined collection of texts written in two languages. The rationale is that named entities such as "Microsoft" or "HIV" are identical in different languages with the same writing system. Using term correlation, the algorithm can identify semantically similar words in both languages. The authors exploit these mappings in cross-lingual topic classification, and their results are promising. However, using bilingual dictionaries as well yields a considerable improvement, as Gliozzo and Strapparava (2006) also report.

While all of the methods above could technically be used in any text classification task, the idiosyncrasies of genres pose additional challenges. Techniques relying on the automated translation of predictive terms (Bel et al., 2003; Prettenhofer and Stein, 2010) are workable in the contexts of topics and sentiment, as these typically rely on content words such as nouns, adjectives, and adverbs. For example, "hospital" may indicate a text from the medical domain, while "excellent" may indicate that a review is positive. Such terms are relatively easy to translate, even if not always without uncertainty. Genres, on the other hand, are often classified using function words (Karlgren and Cutting, 1994; Stamatatos et al., 2000b) like "of", "it", or "in". It is clear that translating these out of context is next to impossible. This is true in particular if there are differences in morphology, since function words in one language may be morphological affixes in another.

Although it is theoretically possible to use the bilingual low-dimension approach by Gliozzo and Strapparava (2006) for genre classification, it relies on certain words to be identical in two different languages. While this may be the case for topic-indicating named entities — a text containing the words "Obama" and "McCain" will almost certainly be about the U.S. elections in 2008, or at least about U.S. politics — there is little indication of what its genre might be: It could be a news report, an editorial, a letter, an interview, a biography, or a blog entry, just to name a few. Because topics and genres correlate, one would probably reject some genres like instruction manuals or fiction novels. However, uncertainty is still large, and Petrenz and Webber (2011) show that it can be dangerous to rely on such correlations. This is particularly true in the cross-lingual case, as it is not clear whether genres and topics correlate in similar ways in a different language.

## 3 Approach

The approach I propose here relies on two strategies I explain below in more detail: *Stable features* and *target language adaptation*. The first is based on the assumption that certain features are indicative of certain genres in more than one language, while the latter is a less restricted way to boost performance, once the language gap has been bridged. Figure 1 illustrates this approach, which is a challenging one, as very little prior knowledge is assumed by the system. On the other hand, in theory it allows any resulting application to be used for a wide range of languages.

### 3.1 Assumption of prior knowledge

Typically, the aim of cross-lingual techniques is to leverage the knowledge present in one language in order to help carry a task in another language, for which such knowledge is not available. In the case of genre classification, this knowledge comprises genre labels of the documents used to train the classification model. My approach requires no labeled data in the target language. This is important, as some domain adaptation algorithms rely on a small set of labeled texts in the target domain.

Cross-lingual methods also often rely on MT, but this effectively restricts them to languages for which MT is sufficiently developed. Apart from the fact that it would be desirable for a cross-lingual genre classifier to work for as many

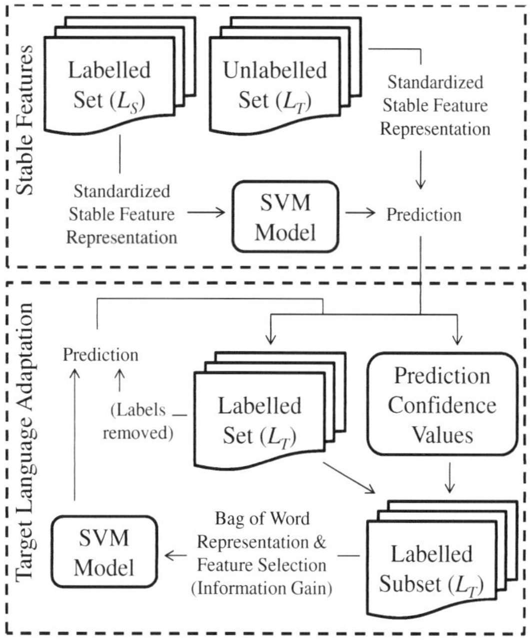


Figure 1: Outline of the proposed method for CLGC.

languages as possible, MT only allows classification in well-resourced languages. However, such languages are more likely to have genre-annotated corpora, and mono-lingual classification may yield better results. In order to bring the advantages of genre classification to poorly-resourced languages, the availability of MT techniques, at least for the time being, must not be assumed. I only use them to generate baseline results.

The same restriction is applied to other types of prior knowledge, and I do not assume supervised PoS taggers, syntactic parsers, or other tools are available. In future work however, I may explore unsupervised methods, such as the PoS induction methods of Clark (2003), Goldwater and Griffiths (2007), or Berg-Kirkpatrick et al. (2010), as they do not represent external knowledge.

There are a few assumptions that must be made in order to carry out any meaningful experiments. First, some way to detect sentence and paragraph boundaries is expected. This can be a simple rule-based algorithm, or unsupervised methods, such as the Punkt boundary detection system by Kiss and Strunk (2006). Also, punctuation symbols and numerals are assumed to be identifiable as such, although their exact semantic function is unknown. For example, a question mark will be identified as a punctuation symbol, but its function (question cue; end of a sentence) will not. Lastly, a sufficiently large, unlabeled set of texts in the target language is required.

### 3.2 Stable features

Many types of features have been used in genre classification. They all fall into one of three groups: *Language-specific features* are cues which can only be extracted from texts in one language. An example would be the frequency of a particular word, such as "yesterday". *Language-independent features* can be extracted in any language, but they are not necessarily directly comparable. Examples would be the frequencies of the ten most common words. While these can be extracted for any language (as long as words can be identified as such), the function of a word on a certain position in this ranking will likely differ from one language to another. *Comparable features*, on the other hand, represent the same function, or part of a function, in two or more languages. An example would be type/token ratios, which, in combination with the document length, represent the lexical richness of a text, independent of its language. If such features prove to be good genre predictors across languages, they may be considered *stable* across those languages. Once suitable features are found, CLGC may be considered a standard classification problem, as outlined in the upper part of Figure 1.

I propose an approach that makes use of such stable features, which include mostly structural, rather than lexical cues (cf. Section 4). Stable features lend themselves to the classification of genres in particular. As already mentioned, genres differ in communicative purpose, rather than in topic. Therefore, features involving content words are only useful to an extent. While topical classification is hard to imagine without translation or parallel/comparable corpora, genre classification can be done without such resources. Stable features provide a way to bridge the language gap even to poorly-resourced languages.

This does not necessarily mean that the values of these attributes are in the same range across languages. For example, the type/token ratio will typically be higher in morphologically-rich languages. However, it might still be true that novels have a richer vocabulary than scientific articles, whether they are written in English or Finnish. In order to exploit such features cross-linguistically, their values have to be mapped from one language to another. This can be done in an unsupervised fashion, as long as enough data is present in both source and target language (cf. Section 3.1). An easy and intuitive way is to standardize values so that each feature in both sets has a mean value of zero mean and variance of one. This is achieved by subtracting from each feature value the mean over all documents and dividing it by the standard deviation.

Note that the training and test sets have to be standardized separately in order for both sets to have the same mean and variance and thus be comparable. This is different from classification tasks where training and test set are assumed to be sampled from the same distribution. Although standardization (or another type of scaling) is often performed in such tasks as well, the scaling factor from the training set would be used to scale the test set (Hsu et al., 2000).

### 3.3 Target language adaptation

Cross-lingual text classification has often been considered a special case of domain adaptation. Semi-supervised methods, such as the expectation-maximization (EM) algorithm (Dempster et al., 1977), have been employed to make use of both labeled data in the source language and unlabeled data in the target language. However, adapting to a different language poses a greater challenge than adapting to different genres, topics, or sources. As the vocabularies have little (if any) overlap, it is not trivial to initially bridge the gap between the domains. Typically, MT would be used to tackle this problem.

Instead, my use of stable features shifts the focus of subsequent domain adaptation to exploiting unlabeled data in the target language to improve prediction accuracy. I refer to this as *target language adaptation* (TLA). The advantage of making this separation is that a different set of features can be used to adapt to the target language. There is no reason to keep the restrictions required for stable features once the language gap has been bridged. In fact, any language-independent feature may be used for this task. The assumption is that the method described in Section 3.2 provides a good but enhanceable result, that is significantly below mono-lingual performance. The resulting decent, though imperfect, labeling of target language texts may be exploited to improve accuracy.

A wide range of possible features lend themselves to TLA. Language-independent features have often been proposed in prior work on genre classification. These include bag-of-words, character n-grams, and PoS frequencies or PoS n-grams, although the latter two would have to be based on the output of unsupervised PoS induction algorithms in this scenario. Alternatively, PoS tags could be approximated by considering the most frequent words as their own tag, as suggested by Sharoff (2007). With appropriate feature sets, iterative algorithms can be used to improve the labeling of the set in the target domain.

The lower part of Figure 1 illustrates the TLA process proposed for CLGC. In each iteration, confidence values obtained from the previous classification model are used to select a subset of labeled texts in the target language. Intuitively, only texts which can be confidently assigned to a certain genre should be used to train a new model. This is particularly true in the first iteration, after the stable feature prediction, as error rates are expected to be high. The size of this subset is increased at each iteration in the process until it comprises all the texts in the test set. A multi-class Support Vector Machine (SVM) in a $k$ genre problem is a combination of $\frac{k\times(k-1)}{2}$ binary classifiers with voting to determine the overall prediction. To compute a confidence value for this prediction, I use the geometric mean $G = (\prod_{i=1}^{n} a_i)^{1/n}$ of the distances from the decision boundary $a_i$ for all the $n$ binary classifiers, which include the winning genre (i.e., $n = k - 1$). The geometric mean heavily penalizes low values, that is small distances to the hyperplane separating two genres. This corresponds to the intuition that there should be a high certainty in any pairwise genre comparison for a high-confidence prediction. Negative distances from the boundary are counted as zero, which reduces the overall confidence to zero. The acquired subset is then transformed to a bag of words representation. Inspired by the approach of Rigutini et al. (2005), the information gain for each feature is computed, and only the highest ranked features are used. A new classification model is trained and used to re-label the target language texts. This process continues until convergence (i.e., labels in two subsequent iterations are identical) or until a pre-defined iteration limit is reached.

# 4 Experiments

## 4.1 Baselines

To verify the proposed approach, I carried out experiments using two publicly available corpora in English and in Chinese. As there is no prior work on CLGC, I chose as baseline an SVM model trained on the source language set using a bag of words representation as features. This had previously been used for this task by Freund et al. (2006) and Sharoff et al. (2010).[1] The texts in the test set were then translated from the target into the source language using *Google translate*[2] and the SVM model was used to predict their genres. I also tested a variant in which the training set was translated into the target language before the feature extraction step, with the test set remaining untranslated. Note that these are somewhat artificial baselines, as MT in reasonable quality is only available for a few selected languages. They are therefore not workable solutions to classify genres in poorly-resourced languages. Thus, even a cross-lingual performance close to these baselines can be considered a success, as long as no MT is used. For reference, I also report the performances of a random guess approach and a classifier labeling each text as the dominant genre class.

With all experiments, results are reported for the test set in the target language. I infer confidence intervals by assuming that the number of misclassifications is approximately normally distributed with mean $\mu = e \times n$ and standard deviation $\sigma = \sqrt{\mu \times (1 - e)}$, where $e$ is the percentage of misclassified instances and $n$ is the size of the test set. I take two classification results to differ significantly only if their 95% confidence intervals (i.e., $\mu \pm 1.96 \times \sigma$) do not overlap.

## 4.2 Data

In line with some of the prior mono-lingual work on genre classification, I used the Brown corpus for my experiments. As illustrated in Table 1, the 500 texts in the corpus are sampled from 15 genres, which can be categorized more broadly into four broad genre categories, and even more broadly into informative and imaginative texts. The second corpus I used was the Lancaster Corpus of Mandarin Chinese (LCMC). In creating the LCMC, the Brown sampling frame was followed very closely and genres within these two corpora are comparable, with the exception of Western Fiction, which was replaced by Martial Arts Fiction in the LCMC. Texts in both corpora are tokenized by word, sentence, and paragraph, and no further pre-processing steps were necessary.

| | | |
|---|---|---|
| Informative | Press (88 texts) | Press: Reportage |
| | | Press: Editorials |
| | | Press: Reviews |
| | Misc. (176 texts) | Religion |
| | | Skills, Trades & Hobbies |
| | | Popular Lore |
| | | Biographies & Essays |
| | Non-Fiction (110 texts) | Reports & Official Documents |
| | | Academic Prose |
| Imaginative | Fiction (126 texts) | General Fiction |
| | | Mystery & Detective Fiction |
| | | Science Fiction |
| | | Adventure & Western Fiction |
| | | Romantic Fiction |
| | | Humor |

Table 1: Genres in the Brown corpus. Categories are identical in the LCMC, except Western Fiction is replaced by Martial Arts Fiction.

Following Karlgren and Cutting (1994), I tested my approach on all three levels of granularity. However, as the 15-genre task yields relatively poor CLGC results (both for my approach and the baselines), I report and discuss only the results of the two and four-genre task here. Improving performance on more fine-grained genres will be subject of future work (cf. Section 6).

## 4.3 Features and Parameters

The stable features used to bridge the language gap are listed in Table 2. Most are simply extractable cues that have been used in mono-lingual genre classification experiments before: Average sentence/paragraph lengths and standard deviations, type/token ratio and numeral/token ratio. To these, I added a ratio of single lines in a text — that is, paragraphs containing no more than one sentence, divided by the sentence count. These are typically headlines, datelines, author names, or other structurally interesting parts. A distribution value indicates how evenly single lines are distributed throughout a text, with high values indicating single lines predominantly occurring at the beginning and/or end of a text.

[1]Other document representations, including character n-grams, were tested, but found to perform worse in this task.

[2]http://translate.google.com

| Features | F | N | P | M | Features | F | N | P | M |
|---|---|---|---|---|---|---|---|---|---|
| Average Sentence | −0.5 | 0.6 | 0.1 | 0.0 | Type/Token | 0.0 | −0.9 | 0.6 | 0.3 |
| Length | −1.0 | 0.5 | 0.0 | 0.3 | Ratio | 0.0 | −0.9 | 0.9 | 0.1 |
| Sentence Length | −0.3 | 0.5 | −0.1 | 0.0 | Numeral/Token | −0.3 | 0.6 | −0.1 | −0.1 |
| Standard Deviation | −0.5 | 0.4 | 0.0 | 0.1 | Ratio | −0.7 | 0.7 | 0.4 | −0.1 |
| Average Paragraph | −0.4 | 0.3 | −0.1 | 0.1 | Single Lines/ | 0.3 | 0.1 | −0.1 | −0.2 |
| Length | −0.4 | 0.4 | −0.6 | 0.4 | Sentence Ratio | 0.0 | −0.3 | 1.1 | −0.4 |
| Paragraph Length | −0.4 | 0.4 | −0.2 | 0.1 | Single Line | −0.3 | 0.2 | 0.0 | 0.1 |
| Standard Deviation | −0.1 | 0.4 | −0.6 | 0.1 | Distribution | 0.1 | −0.1 | 0.1 | 0.0 |
| Relative tf-idf values of | 0.2 | 0.1 | −0.1 | 0.0 | Topic Average | −0.4 | 0.8 | −0.3 | 0.0 |
| top 10 weighted words* | 0.4 | −0.2 | −0.5 | 0.1 | Precision | −0.4 | 0.8 | −0.2 | −0.1 |

Table 2: Set of 19 stable features used to bridge the language gap. The numbers denote the mean values after standardization for each broad genre in the LCMC (upper values) and Brown corpus (lower values): **F**iction, **N**on-Fiction, **P**ress, and **M**iscellaneous. Negative/Positive numbers denote lower/higher average feature values for this genre when compared to the rest of the corpus. *Relative tf-idf values are ten separate features. The numbers given are for the highest ranked word only.

The remaining features (cf. last row of Table 2) are based on ideas from information retrieval. I used tf-idf weighting and marked the ten highest weighted words in a text as relevant. I then treated this text as a ranked list of relevant and non-relevant words, where the position of a word in the text determined its rank. This allowed me to compute an average precision (AP) value. The intuition behind this value is that genre conventions dictate the location of important content words within a text. A high AP score means that the top tf-idf weighted words are found predominantly in the beginning of a text. In addition, for the same ten words, I added the tf-idf value to the feature set, divided by the sum of all ten. These values indicate whether a text is very focused (a sharp drop between higher and lower ranked words) or more spread out across topics (relatively flat distribution).

For each of these features, Table 2 shows the mean values for the four broad genre classes in the LCMC and Brown corpus, after the sets have been standardized to zero mean and unit variance. This is the same preprocessing process used for training and testing the SVM model, although the statistics in Table 2 are not available to the classifier, since they require genre labels. Each row gives an idea of how suitable a feature might be to distinguish between these genres in Chinese (upper row) and English (lower row). Both rows together indicate how stable a feature is across languages for this task. Some features, such as the topic AP value, seems to be both a good predictor for genre and stable across languages. In both Chinese and English, for example, the topical words seem to be concentrated around the beginning of the text in Non-Fiction, but much less so in Fiction. These patterns can be seen in other features as well. The type/token ratio is, on average, highest in Press texts, followed by Miscellaneous texts, Fiction texts, and Non-Fiction texts in both corpora. While this does not hold for all the features, many such patterns can be observed in Table 2.

Since uncertainty after the initial prediction is very high, the subset used to re-train the SVM model was chosen to be small. In the first iteration, I used up to 60% of texts with the highest confidence value within each genre. To avoid an imbalanced class distribution, texts were chosen so that the genre distribution in the new training set matched the one in the source language. To illustrate this, consider an example with two genre classes A and B, represented by 80% and 20% of texts respectively in the source language. Assuming that after the initial prediction both classes are assigned to 100 texts in a test set of size 200, the 60 texts with the highest confidence values would be chosen for class A. To keep the genre distribution of the source language, only the top 15 texts would be chosen for class B.

In the second iteration, I simply used the top 90% of texts overall. This number was increased by 5% in each subsequent iteration, so that the full set was used from the fourth iteration. No changes were made to the genre distribution from the second iteration. To train the classification model, I used the 500 features with the highest informa-

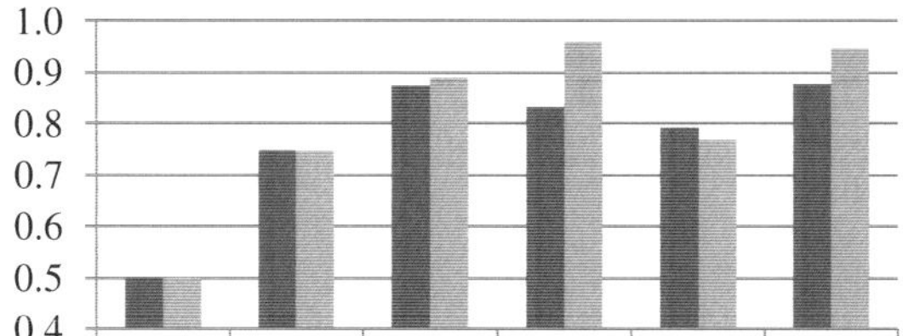


| | Rand. | Prior | MT Source | MT Target | SF | SF + TLA |
|---|---|---|---|---|---|---|
| t: zh | 50.0% | 74.8% | 87.2% | 83.2% | 79.2% | 87.6% |
| t: en | 50.0% | 74.8% | 88.8% | 95.8% | 76.8% | 94.6% |

Figure 2: Prediction accuracies for the Brown / LCMC two genre classification task. Dark bars denote English as source language and Chinese as target language (en→zh), light bars denote the reverse (zh→en). Rand.: Random classifier. Prior: Classifier always predicting the most dominant class. The baselines MT Source and MT target use MT to translate texts into the source and target language, respectively. SF: Stable Features. TLA: Target Language Adaptation.

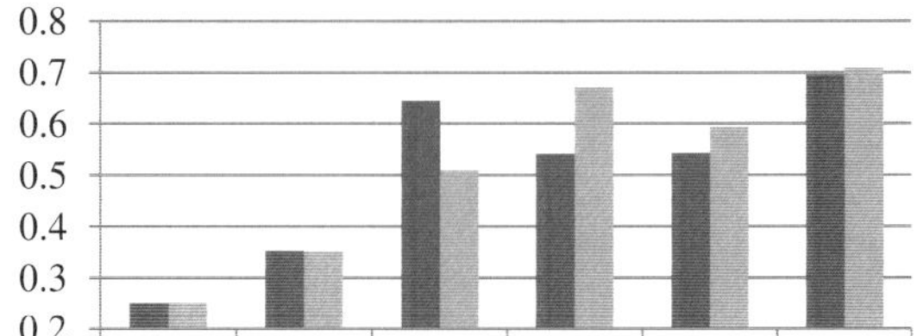


| | Rand. | Prior | MT Source | MT Target | SF | SF + TLA |
|---|---|---|---|---|---|---|
| t: zh | 25.0% | 35.2% | 64.4% | 54.0% | 54.2% | 69.4% |
| t: en | 25.0% | 35.2% | 51.0% | 66.8% | 59.2% | 70.8% |

Figure 3: Prediction accuracies for the Brown / LCMC four genre classification task. Labels as in Figure 2.

tion gain score for the selected training set in each iteration. As convergence is not guaranteed theoretically, I used a maximum limit of 15 iterations. In my experiments however, the algorithm always converged.

## 5 Results and Discussion

Figure 2 shows the accuracies for the two genre task (informative texts vs. imaginative texts) in both directions: English as a source language with Chinese being the target language (en→zh) and vice versa (zh→en). As the class distribution is skewed (374 vs. 126 texts), always predicting the most dominant class yields acceptable performance. However, this is simplistic and might fail in practice, where the most dominant class will typically be unknown.

Full text translation combined with monolingual classification performs well. Stable features alone yield a respectable prediction accuracy, but perform significantly worse than MT Source in both tasks and MT Target in the zh→en task. However, subsequent TLA significantly improves the accuracy on both tasks, eliminating any significant difference from baseline performance.

Figure 3 shows results for the four genre classification task (Fiction vs. Non-Fiction vs. Press vs. Misc.). Again, MT Source and MT Target perform well. However, translating from Chinese into English yields better results than the reverse. This might be due to the easier identification of words in English and thus a more accurate bag of words representation. TLA manages to significantly improve the stable feature results. My approach outperforms both baselines in this experiment, although the differences are only significant if texts are translated from English to Chinese.

These results are encouraging, as they show that in CLGC tasks, equal or better performance can be achieved with fewer resources, when compared the baseline of full text translation. The reason why TLA works well in this case can be understood by comparing the confusion matrices before the first iteration and after convergence (Table 3). While it is obvious that the stable feature approach works better on some classes than on others, the distributions of predicted and actual genres are fairly similar. For Fiction, Non-Fiction, and Press, precision is above 50%, with correct predictions outweighing incorrect ones, which is an important basis for subsequent iterative learning. However, too many texts are predicted to belong to the Miscellaneous category, which reduces recall on the other genres. By using a different feature set and concentrating on the documents with high confidence values, TLA manages to remedy this problem to an extent. While misclassifications are still present, recalls for the Fiction and Non-Fiction genres are increased significantly, which explains the higher overall accuracy.

## 6 Conclusion and future work

I have presented the first work on cross-lingual genre classification (CLGC). I have shown that some text features can be considered stable genre predictors across languages and that it is possible to achieve good results in CLGC tasks without

| | Fict. | Non-Fict. | Press | Misc. |
|---|---|---|---|---|
| Fiction | 65 | 2 | 8 | 51 |
| Non-Fiction | 4 | 59 | 2 | 45 |
| Press | 5 | 8 | 31 | 44 |
| Miscellaneous | 18 | 28 | 14 | 116 |
| Precision | 0.71 | 0.61 | 0.56 | 0.45 |
| Recall | 0.52 | 0.54 | 0.35 | 0.66 |

| | Fict. | Non-Fict. | Press | Misc. |
|---|---|---|---|---|
| Fiction | 102 | 0 | 2 | 22 |
| Non-Fiction | 0 | 83 | 0 | 27 |
| Press | 2 | 8 | 27 | 51 |
| Miscellaneous | 29 | 9 | 3 | 135 |
| Precision | 0.77 | 0.83 | 0.84 | 0.57 |
| Recall | 0.81 | 0.75 | 0.31 | 0.77 |

Table 3: Confusion Matrices for the four genre en→zh task. Left: After stable feature prediction, but before TLA. Right: After TLA convergence. Rows 2–5 denote actual numbers of texts, columns denote predictions.

resource-intensive MT techniques. My approach exploits stable features to bridge the language gap and subsequently applies iterative target language adaptation (TLA) in order to improve accuracy. The approach performed equally well or better than full text translation combined with monolingual classification. Considering that English and Chinese are very dissimilar linguistically, I expect the approach to work at least equally well for more closely related language pairs.

This work is still in progress. While my results are encouraging, more work is needed to make the CLGC approach more robust. At the moment, classification accuracy is low for problems with many classes. I plan to remedy this by implementing a hierarchical classification framework, where a text is assigned a broad genre label first and then classified further within this category.

Since TLA can only work on a sufficiently good initial labeling of target language texts, stable feature classification results have to be improved as well. To this end, I propose to focus initially on features involving punctuation. This could include analyses of the different punctuation symbols used in comparison with the rest of the document set, their frequencies and deviations between sentences, punctuation n-gram patterns, as well as the analyses of the positions of punctuation symbols within sentences or whole texts. Punctuation has frequently been used in genre classification tasks and it is expected that some of the features based on such symbols are valuable in a cross-lingual setting as well. As vocabulary richness seems to be a useful predictor of genres, experiments will also be extended beyond the simple inclusion of type/token ratios in the feature set. For example, *hapax legomena* statistics could be used, as well as the conformance to text laws, such as Zipf, Benford, and Heaps.

After this, I will examine text structure a predictor. While single line statistics and topic AP scores already reflect text structure, more sophisticated pre-processing methods, such as text segmentation and unsupervised PoS induction, might yield better results. The experiments using the tf-idf values of terms will be extended. Resulting features may include the positions of highly weighted words in a text, the amount of topics covered, or identification of summaries.

TLA techniques can also be refined. An obvious choice is to consider different types of features, as mentioned in Section 3.3. Different representations may even be combined to capture the notion of different communicative purpose, similar to the multi-dimensional approach by Biber (1995). An interesting idea to combine different sets of features was suggested by Chaker and Habib (2007). Assigning a document to all genres with different probabilities and repeating this for different sets of features may yield a very flexible classifier. The impact of the feature sets on the final prediction could be weighted according to different criteria, such as prediction certainty or overlap with other feature sets. Improvements may also be achieved by choosing a more reliable method for finding the most confident genre predictions as a function of the distance to the SVM decision boundary. Cross-validation techniques will be explored to estimate confidence values.

Finally, I will have to test the approach on a larger set of data with texts from more languages. To this end, I am working to compile a reference corpus for CLGC by combining publicly available sources. This would be useful to compare methods and will hopefully encourage further research.

## Acknowledgments

I thank Bonnie Webber, Benjamin Rosman, and three anonymous reviewers for their helpful comments on an earlier version of this paper.

## References


Shlomo Argamon, Moshe Koppel, and Galit Avneri. 1998. Routing documents according to style. In *Proceedings of First International Workshop on Innovative Information Systems*.

Nuria Bel, Cornelis Koster, and Marta Villegas. 2003. Cross-lingual text categorization. In Traugott Koch and Ingeborg Slvberg, editors, *Research and Advanced Technology for Digital Libraries*, volume 2769 of *Lecture Notes in Computer Science*, pages 126–139. Springer Berlin / Heidelberg.

Taylor Berg-Kirkpatrick, Alexandre Bouchard-Côté, John DeNero, and Dan Klein. 2010. Painless unsupervised learning with features. In *Human Language Technologies: The 2010 Annual Conference of the North American Chapter of the Association for Computational Linguistics*, HLT '10, pages 582–590, Stroudsburg, PA, USA. Association for Computational Linguistics.

Douglas Biber. 1988. *Variation across Speech and Writing*. Cambridge University Press, Cambridge.

Douglas Biber. 1995. *Dimensions of Register Variation*. Cambridge University Press, New York.

Pavel Braslavski. 2004. Document style recognition using shallow statistical analysis. In *Proceedings of the ESSLLI 2004 Workshop on Combining Shallow and Deep Processing for NLP*, pages 1–9.

Jebari Chaker and Ounelli Habib. 2007. Genre categorization of web pages. In *Proceedings of the Seventh IEEE International Conference on Data Mining Workshops*, ICDMW '07, pages 455–464, Washington, DC, USA. IEEE Computer Society.

Alexander Clark. 2003. Combining distributional and morphological information for part of speech induction. In *Proceedings of the tenth conference on European chapter of the Association for Computational Linguistics - Volume 1*, EACL '03, pages 59–66, Stroudsburg, PA, USA. Association for Computational Linguistics.

O. de Vel, A. Anderson, M. Corney, and G. Mohay. 2001. Mining e-mail content for author identification forensics. *SIGMOD Rec.*, 30(4):55–64.

A. P. Dempster, N. M. Laird, and D. B. Rubin. 1977. Maximum Likelihood from Incomplete Data via the EM Algorithm. *Journal of the Royal Statistical Society. Series B (Methodological)*, 39(1):1–38.

S. Feldman, M. A. Marin, M. Ostendorf, and M. R. Gupta. 2009. Part-of-speech histograms for genre classification of text. In *Proceedings of the 2009 IEEE International Conference on Acoustics, Speech and Signal Processing*, pages 4781–4784, Washington, DC, USA. IEEE Computer Society.

Aidan Finn and Nicholas Kushmerick. 2006. Learning to classify documents according to genre. *J. Am. Soc. Inf. Sci. Technol.*, 57(11):1506–1518.

Luanne Freund, Charles L. A. Clarke, and Elaine G. Toms. 2006. Towards genre classification for IR in the workplace. In *Proceedings of the 1st international conference on Information interaction in context*, pages 30–36, New York, NY, USA. ACM.

Alfio Gliozzo and Carlo Strapparava. 2006. Exploiting comparable corpora and bilingual dictionaries for cross-language text categorization. In *Proceedings of the 21st International Conference on Computational Linguistics and the 44th annual meeting of the Association for Computational Linguistics*, ACL-44, pages 553–560, Stroudsburg, PA, USA. Association for Computational Linguistics.

Jade Goldstein, Gary M. Ciany, and Jaime G. Carbonell. 2007. Genre identification and goal-focused summarization. In *Proceedings of the sixteenth ACM conference on Conference on information and knowledge management*, CIKM '07, pages 889–892, New York, NY, USA. ACM.

Sharon Goldwater and Tom Griffiths. 2007. A fully Bayesian approach to unsupervised part-of-speech tagging. In *Proceedings of the 45th Annual Meeting of the Association of Computational Linguistics*, pages 744–751, Prague, Czech Republic, June. Association for Computational Linguistics.

Chih-Wei Hsu, Chih-Chung Chang, and Chih-Jen Lin. 2000. A Practical Guide to Support Vector Classification.

Thorsten Joachims. 1998. Text categorization with suport vector machines: Learning with many relevant features. In *Proceedings of the 10th European Conference on Machine Learning*, pages 137–142, London, UK. Springer-Verlag.

Ioannis Kanaris and Efstathios Stamatatos. 2007. Webpage genre identification using variable-length character n-grams. In *Proceedings of the 19th IEEE International Conference on Tools with AI*, pages 3–10, Washington, DC.

Jussi Karlgren and Douglass Cutting. 1994. Recognizing text genres with simple metrics using discriminant analysis. In *Proceedings of the 15th Conference on Computational Linguistics*, pages 1071–1075, Morristown, NJ, USA. Association for Computational Linguistics.

Brett Kessler, Geoffrey Nunberg, and Hinrich Schütze. 1997. Automatic detection of text genre. In *Proceedings of the 35th Annual Meeting of the Association for Computational Linguistics*, pages 32–38, Morristown, NJ, USA. Association for Computational Linguistics.

Yunhyong Kim and Seamus Ross. 2008. Examining variations of prominent features in genre classification. In *Proceedings of the Proceedings of the 41st Annual Hawaii International Conference on System Sciences*, HICSS '08, pages 132–, Washington, DC, USA. IEEE Computer Society.

Tibor Kiss and Jan Strunk. 2006. Unsupervised multilingual sentence boundary detection. *Comput. Linguist.*, 32:485–525, December.

Jon Oberlander and Scott Nowson. 2006. Whose thumb is it anyway?: classifying author personality from weblog text. In *Proceedings of the COLING/ACL on Main conference poster sessions*, COLING-ACL '06, pages 627–634, Morristown, NJ, USA. Association for Computational Linguistics.

Bo Pang, Lillian Lee, and Shivakumar Vaithyanathan. 2002. Thumbs up?: sentiment classification using machine learning techniques. In *Proceedings of the ACL-02 conference on Empirical methods in natural language processing - Volume 10*, EMNLP '02, pages 79–86, Morristown, NJ, USA. Association for Computational Linguistics.

Philipp Petrenz and Bonnie Webber. 2011. Stable classification of text genres. *Comput. Linguist.*, 37:385–393.

Peter Prettenhofer and Benno Stein. 2010. Cross-language text classification using structural correspondence learning. In *Proceedings of the 48th Annual Meeting of the Association for Computational Linguistics*, ACL '10, pages 1118–1127, Stroudsburg, PA, USA. Association for Computational Linguistics.

Leonardo Rigutini, Marco Maggini, and Bing Liu. 2005. An em based training algorithm for cross-language text categorization. In *Proceedings of the Web Intelligence Conference*, pages 529–535.

Evan Sandhaus. 2008. New York Times corpus: Corpus overview. LDC catalogue entry LDC2008T19.

Fabrizio Sebastiani. 2002. Machine learning in automated text categorization. *ACM Comput. Surv.*, 34:1–47, March.

Serge Sharoff, Zhili Wu, and Katja Markert. 2010. The Web Library of Babel: Evaluating genre collections. In *Proceedings of the Seventh conference on International Language Resources and Evaluation*, pages 3063–3070, Valletta, Malta, may. European Language Resources Association (ELRA).

Serge Sharoff. 2007. Classifying web corpora into domain and genre using automatic feature identification. In *Proceedings of Web as Corpus Workshop*.

E. Stamatatos, N. Fakotakis, and G. Kokkinakis. 2000a. Text genre detection using common word frequencies. In *Proceedings of the 18th conference on Computational linguistics*, pages 808–814, Morristown, NJ, USA. Association for Computational Linguistics.

Efstathios Stamatatos, George Kokkinakis, and Nikos Fakotakis. 2000b. Automatic text categorization in terms of genre and author. *Computational Linguistics*, 26(4):471–495.

Xiaojun Wan. 2009. Co-training for cross-lingual sentiment classification. In *Proceedings of the Joint Conference of the 47th Annual Meeting of the ACL and the 4th International Joint Conference on Natural Language Processing of the AFNLP: Volume 1 - Volume 1*, ACL '09, pages 235–243, Stroudsburg, PA, USA. Association for Computational Linguistics.

Bonnie Webber. 2009. Genre distinctions for discourse in the Penn TreeBank. In *Proceedings of the Joint Conference of the 47th Annual Meeting of the ACL and the 4th International Joint Conference on Natural Language Processing of the AFNLP*, pages 674–682.

Maria Wolters and Mathias Kirsten. 1999. Exploring the use of linguistic features in domain and genre classification. In *Proceedings of the ninth conference on European chapter of the Association for Computational Linguistics*, EACL '99, pages 142–149, Stroudsburg, PA, USA. Association for Computational Linguistics.

# A Comparative Study of Reinforcement Learning Techniques on Dialogue Management

**Alexandros Papangelis**
NCSR "Demokritos",
Institute of Informatics
& Telecommunications
and
Univ. of Texas at Arlington,
Comp. Science and Engineering
alexandros.papangelis@mavs.uta.edu

## Abstract

Adaptive Dialogue Systems are rapidly becoming part of our everyday lives. As they progress and adopt new technologies they become more intelligent and able to adapt better and faster to their environment. Research in this field is currently focused on how to achieve adaptation, and particularly on applying Reinforcement Learning (RL) techniques, so a comparative study of the related methods, such as this, is necessary. In this work we compare several standard and state of the art online RL algorithms that are used to train the dialogue manager in a dynamic environment, aiming to aid researchers / developers choose the appropriate RL algorithm for their system. This is the first work, to the best of our knowledge, to evaluate online RL algorithms on the dialogue problem and in a dynamic environment.

## 1 Introduction

Dialogue Systems (DS) are systems that are able to make natural conversation with their users. There are many types of DS that serve various aims, from hotel and flight booking to providing information or keeping company and forming long term relationships with the users. Other interesting types of DS are tutorial systems, whose goal is to teach something new, persuasive systems whose goal is to affect the user's attitude towards something through casual conversation and rehabilitation systems that aim at engaging patients to various activities that help their rehabilitation process. DS that incorporate adaptation to their environment are called Adaptive Dialogue Systems (ADS). Over the past few years ADS have seen a lot of progress and have attracted the research community's and industry's interest.

There is a number of available ADS, applying state of the art techniques for adaptation and learning, such as the one presented by Young et al., (2010), where the authors propose an ADS that provides tourist information in a fictitious town. Their system is trained using RL and some clever state compression techniques to make it scalable, it is robust to noise and able to recover from errors (misunderstandings). Cuayáhuitl et al. (2010) propose a travel planning ADS, that is able to learn dialogue policies using RL, building on top of existing handcrafted policies. This enables the designers of the system to provide prior knowledge and the system can then learn the details. Konstantopoulos (2010) proposes an affective ADS which serves as a museum guide. It is able to adapt to each user's personality by assessing his / her emotional state and current mood and also adapt its output to the user's expertise level. The system itself has an emotional state that is affected by the user and affects its output.

An example ADS architecture is depicted in Figure 1, where we can see several components trying to understand the user's utterance and several others trying to express the system's response. The system first attempts to convert spoken input to text using the Automatic Speech Recognition (ASR) component and then tries to infer the meaning using the Natural Language Understanding (NLU) component. At the core lies the Dialogue Manager (DM), a component responsible for understanding what the user's utterance means and deciding which action to take that will lead to achieving his / her goals. The DM may also take into account contextual information

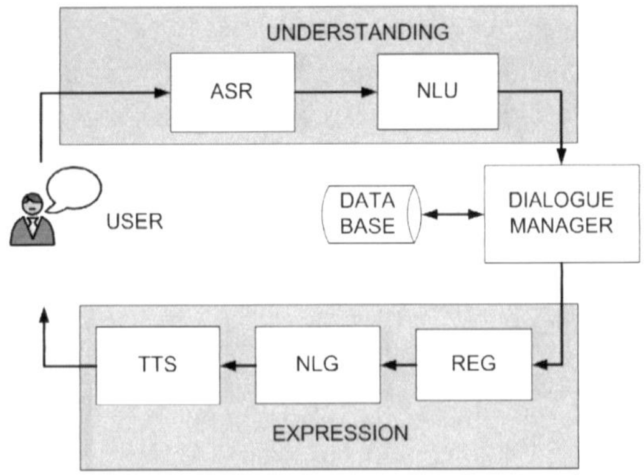


Figure 1: Example architecture of an ADS.

or historical data before making a decision. After the system has decided what to say, it uses the Referring Expression Generation (REG) component to create appropriate referring expressions, the Natural Language Generation (NLG) component to create the textual form of the output and last, the Text To Speech (TTS) component to convert the text to spoken output.

Trying to make ADS as human-like as possible researchers have focused on techniques that achieve adaptation, i.e. adjust to the current user's personality, behaviour, mood, needs and to the environment in general. Examples include adaptive or trainable NLG (Rieser and Lemon, 2009), where the authors formulate their problem as a statistical planning problem and use RL to find a policy according to which the system will decide how to present information. Another example is adaptive REG (Janarthanam and Lemon, 2009), where the authors again use RL to choose one of three strategies (jargon, tutorial, descriptive) according to the user's expertise level. An example of adaptive TTS is the work of Boidin et al. (2009), where the authors propose a model that sorts paraphrases with respect to predictions of which sounds more natural. Jurčíček et al. (2010) propose a RL algorithm to optimize ADS parameters in general. Last, many researchers have used RL to achieve adaptive Dialogue Management (Pietquin and Hastie, 2011; Gašić et al., 2010; Cuayáhuitl et al., 2010).

As the reader may have noticed, the current trend in training these components is the application of RL techniques. RL is a well established field of artificial intelligence and provides us with robust frameworks that are able to deal with uncertainty and can scale to real world problems. One sub category of RL is Online RL where the system can be trained on the fly, as it interacts with its environment. These techniques have recently begun to be applied to Dialogue Management and in this paper we perform an extensive evaluation of several standard and state of the art Online RL techniques on a generic dialogue problem. Our experiments were conducted with user simulations, with or without noise and using a model that is able to alter the user's needs at any given point. We were thus able to see how well each algorithm adapted to minor (noise / uncertainty) or major (change in user needs) changes in the environment.

In general, RL algorithms fall in two categories, planning and learning algorithms. Planning or model-based algorithms use training examples from previous interactions with the environment as well as a model of the environment that simulates interactions. Learning or model-free algorithms only use training examples from previous interactions with the environment and that is the main difference of these two categories, according to Sutton and Barto, (1998). The goal of an RL algorithm is to learn a good policy (or strategy) that dictates how the system should interact with the environment. An algorithm then can follow a specific policy (i.e. interact with the environment in a specific, maybe predefined, way) while searching for a good policy. This way of learning is called "off policy" learning. The opposite is "on policy" learning, when the algorithm follows the policy that it is trying to learn. This will become clear in section 2.2 where we provide the basics of RL. Last, these algorithms can be categorized as policy iteration or value iteration algorithms, according to the way they evaluate and train a policy.

Table 1 shows the algorithms we evaluated along with some of their characteristics. We selected representative algorithms for each category and used the Dyna architecture (Sutton and Barto, 1998) to implement model based algorithms.

SARSA($\lambda$) (Sutton and Barto, 1998), Q Learning (Watkins, 1989), Q($\lambda$) (Watkins, 1989; Peng and Williams, 1996) and AC-QV (Wiering and Van Hasselt, 2009) are well established RL algorithms, proven to work and simple to implement. A serious disadvantage though is the fact that they do not scale well (assuming we have enough memory), as also supported by our results in section 5. Least Squares SARSA($\lambda$) (Chen and Wei, 2008) is a variation of SARSA($\lambda$) that uses the least squares method to find the optimal policy. Incremental Actor Critic (IAC) (Bhatnagar et al., 2007) and Natural Actor Critic (NAC) (Peters et al., 2005) are actor - critic algorithms that follow the expected rewards gradient and the natural or Fisher Information gradient respectively (Szepesvári, 2010).

An important attribute of many learning algorithms is function approximation which allows them to scale to real world problems. Function approximation attempts to approximate a target function by selecting from a class of functions that closely resembles the target. Care must be taken however, when applying this method, because many RL algorithms are not guaranteed to converge when using function approximation. On the other hand, policy gradient algorithms (algorithms that perform gradient ascend/descend on a performance surface), such as NAC or Natural Actor Belief Critic (Jurčíček et al., 2010) have good guarantees for convergence, even if we use function approximation (Bhatnagar et al., 2007).

| *Algorithm* | Model | Policy | Iteration |
|---|---|---|---|
| SARSA($\lambda$) | No | On | Value |
| LS-SARSA($\lambda$) | No | On | Policy |
| Q Learning | No | Off | Value |
| Q($\lambda$) | No | Off | Value |
| Actor Critic - QV | No | On | Policy |
| IAC | No | On | Policy |
| NAC | No | On | Policy |
| DynaSARSA($\lambda$) | Yes | On | Value |
| DynaQ | Yes | Off | Value |
| DynaQ($\lambda$) | Yes | Off | Value |
| DynaAC-QV | Yes | On | Policy |

Table 1: Online RL algorithms used in our evaluation.

While there is a significant amount of work in evaluating RL algorithms, this is the first attempt, to the best of our knowledge, to evaluate online learning RL algorithms on the dialogue management problem, in the presence of uncertainty and changes in the environment.

Atkeson and Santamaria (1997) evaluate model based and model free algorithms on the single pendulum swingup problem but their algorithms are not the ones we have selected and the problem on which they were evaluated differs from ours in many ways. Ross et al. (2008) compare many online planning algorithms for solving Partially Observable Markov Decision Processes (POMDP). It is a comprehensive study but not directly related to ours, as we model our problem with Markov Decision Processes (MDP) and evaluate model-based and model-free algorithms on a specific task.

In the next section we provide some background knowledge on MDPs and RL techniques, in section 3 we present our proposed formulation of the slot filling dialogue problem, in section 4 we describe our experimental setup and results, in section 5 we discuss those results and in section 6 we conclude this study.

## 2 Background

In order to fully understand the concepts discussed in this work we will briefly introduce MDP and RL and explain how these techniques can be applied to the dialogue policy learning problem.

### 2.1 Markov Decision Process

A MDP is defined as a triplet $M = \{X, A, P\}$, where $X$ is a non empty set of states, $A$ is a non empty set of actions and $P$ is a transition probability kernel that assigns probability measures over $X \times \mathbb{R}$ for each state-action pair $(x, a) \in X \times A$. We can also define the state transition probability kernel $P_t$ that for each triplet $(x_1, a, x_2) \in X \times A \times X$ would give us the probability of moving from state $x_1$ to state $x_2$ by taking action $a$. Each transition from a state to another is associated with an immediate reward, the expected value of which is called the reward function and is defined as $R(x, a) = \mathbb{E}[r(x, a)]$, where $r(x, a)$ is the immediate reward the system receives after taking action $a$ (Szepesvári, 2010). An episodic MDP is defined as an MDP with terminal states, $X_{t+s} = x, \forall s > 1$. We consider an episode over when a terminal state is reached.

### 2.2 Reinforcement Learning

Motivation to use RL in the dialogue problem came from the fact that it can easily tackle some of the challenges that arise when implementing dialogue systems. One of those, for example, is error recovery. Hand crafted error recovery does not scale at all so we need an automated process to learn error-recovery strategies. More than this we can automatically learn near optimal dialogue policies and thus maximize user satisfaction. Another benefit of RL is that it can be trained using either real or simulated users and continue to learn and adapt with each interaction (in the case of online learning). To use RL we need to model the dialogue system using MDPs, POMDPs or Semi Markov Desicion Processes (SMDP). POMDPs take uncertainty into account and model each state with a distribution that represents our belief that the system is in a specific state. SMDPs add temporal abstraction to the model and allow for time consuming operations. We, however, do not deal with either of those in an attempt to keep the problem simple and focus on the task of comparing the algorithms.

More formally, RL tries to maximize an objective function by learning how to control the actions of a system. A system in this setting is typically formulated as an MDP. As we discussed in section 2.1 for every MDP we can define a policy $\pi$, which is a mapping from states $x \in X$ and actions $\alpha \in A$ to a distribution $\pi(x, \alpha)$ that represents the probability of taking action $\alpha$ when the system is in state $x$. This policy dictates the behaviour of the system. To estimate how good a policy is we define the *value function* $V$:

$$V^{\pi}(x) = \mathbb{E}[\sum_{t=0}^{\infty} \gamma^t R_{t+1} | x_0 = x], x \in X \quad (1)$$

which gives us the expected cumulative rewards when beginning from state $x$ and following policy $\pi$, discounted by a factor $\gamma \in [0, 1]$ that models the importance of future rewards. We define the *return* of a policy $\pi$ as:

$$J^{\pi} = \sum_{t=0}^{\infty} \gamma^t R_t(x_t, \pi(x_t)) \quad (2)$$

A policy $\pi$ is optimal if $J^{\pi}(x) = V^{\pi}(x), \forall x \in X$. We can also define the *action-value function* $Q$:

$$Q^{\pi}(x, \alpha) = \mathbb{E}[\sum_{t=0}^{\infty} \gamma^t R_{t+1} | x_0 = x, a_0 = \alpha] \quad (3)$$

where $x \in X, \alpha \in A$, which gives us the expected cumulative discounted rewards when beginning from state $x$ and taking action $\alpha$, again following policy $\pi$. Note that $V_{max} = \frac{r_{max}}{1-\gamma}$, where $R(x) \in [r_{min}, r_{max}]$.

The goal of RL therefore is to find the optimal policy, which maximizes either of these functions (Szepesvári, 2010).

## 3 Slot Filling Problem

We formulated the problem as a generic slot filling ADS, represented as an MDP. This model has been proposed in (Papangelis et al., 2012), and we extend it here to account for uncertainty. Formally the problem is defined as: $S = < s_0, ..., s_N > \in M, M = M_0 \times M_1 \times ... \times M_N, M_i = \{1, ..., T_i\}$, where $S$ are the $N$ slots to be filled, each slot $s_i$ can take values from $M_i$ and $T_i$ is the number of available values slot $s_i$ can be filled with. Dialogue state is also defined as a vector $d \in M$, where each dimension corresponds to a slot and its value corresponds to the slot's value. We call the set of all possible dialogue states $D$. System actions $A \in \{1, ..., |S|\}$ are defined as requests for slots to be filled and $a_i$ requests slot $s_i$. At each dialogue state $d_i$ we define a set of available actions $\tilde{a}_i \subset A$. A user query $q \subset S$ is defined as the slots that need to be filled so that the system will be able to accurately provide an answer. We assume action $a_N$ always means *Give Answer*. The reward function is defined as:

$$R(d, a) = \begin{cases} -1, & \text{if} \quad a \neq a_N \\ -100, & \text{if} \quad a = a_N, \exists q_i | q_i = \emptyset \\ 0, & \text{if} \quad a = a_N, \neg \exists q_i | q_i = \emptyset \end{cases} \quad (4)$$

Thus, the optimal reward for each problem is $-|q|$ since $|q| < |S|$.

Available actions for every state can be modelled as a matrix $\tilde{A} \in \{0, 1\}^{|D| \times |A|}$, where:

$$\tilde{A}_{ij} = \begin{cases} 1, & \text{if} \quad a_j \in \tilde{a}_i \\ 0, & \text{if} \quad a_j \notin \tilde{a}_i \end{cases} \quad (5)$$

When designing $\tilde{A}$ one must keep in mind that the optimal solution depends on $\tilde{A}$'s structure and must take care not to create an unsolvable problem, i.e. a disconnected MDP. This can be avoided by making sure that each action is available at some state and that each state has at least one available action. We should now define the necessary conditions for the slot filling problem to be solvable and the optimal reward be as defined before:

$$\exists \tilde{\alpha}_{ij} = 1, \quad 1 \leq i < |D|, \forall j \quad (6)$$

$$\exists\tilde{\alpha}_{ij} = 1, \quad 1 < j < |A|, \forall i \tag{7}$$

Note that $j > 1$ since $d_1$ is our starting state. We also allow *Give Answer* (which is $a_N$) to be available from any state:

$$\tilde{A}_{i,N} = 1, \quad 1 \leq i \leq |D| \tag{8}$$

We define available action density to be the ratio of 1s over the number of elements of $\tilde{A}$:

$$Density = \frac{|\{(i,j)|\tilde{A}_{ij} = 1\}|}{|D| \times |A|}$$

We can now incorporate uncertainty in our model. Rather than allowing deterministic transitions from a state to another we define a distribution $P_t(d_j|d_i, a_m)$ which models the probability by which the system will go from state $d_i$ to $d_j$ when taking action $a_m$. Consequently, when the system takes action $a_m$ from state $d_i$, it transits to state $d_k$ with probability:

$$P_t(d_k|d_i, a_m) = \begin{cases} P_t(d_j|d_i, a_m), & k = j \\ \frac{1-P_t(d_j|d_i,a_m)}{|D|-1}, & k \neq j \end{cases} \tag{9}$$

assuming that under no noise conditions action $a_m$ would move the system from state $d_i$ to state $d_j$. The probability of not transiting to state $d_j$ is uniformly distributed among all other states. $P_t(d_j|d_i, a_m)$ is updated after each episode with a small additive noise $\nu$, mainly to model undesirable or unforeseen effects of actions. Another distribution, $P_c(s_j = 1) \in [0, 1]$, models our confidence level that slot $s_j$ is filled:

$$s_j = \begin{cases} 1, & P_c(s_j = 1) \geq 0.5 \\ 0, & P_c(s_j = 1) < 0.5 \end{cases} \tag{10}$$

In our evaluation $P_c(s_j)$ is a random number between $[1 - \epsilon, 1]$ where $\epsilon$ models the level of uncertainty. Last, we can slightly alter $\tilde{A}$ after each episode to model changes or faults in the available actions for each state, but we did not in our experiments.

The algorithms selected for this evaluation are then called to solve this problem online and find an optimal policy $\pi^\star$ that will yield the highest possible reward.

| *Algorithm* | $\alpha$ | $\beta$ | $\gamma$ | $\lambda$ |
|---|---|---|---|---|
| SARSA($\lambda$) | 0.95 | - | 0.55 | 0.4 |
| LS-SARSA($\lambda$) | 0.95 | - | 0.55 | 0.4 |
| Q Learning | 0.8 | - | 0.8 | - |
| Q($\lambda$) | 0.8 | - | 0.8 | 0.05 |
| Actor Critic - QV | 0.9 | 0.25 | 0.75 | - |
| IAC | 0.9 | 0.25 | 0.75 | - |
| NAC | 0.9 | 0.25 | 0.75 | - |
| DynaSARSA($\lambda$) | 0.95 | - | 0.25 | 0.25 |
| DynaQ | 0.8 | - | 0.4 | - |
| DynaQ($\lambda$) | 0.8 | - | 0.4 | 0.05 |
| DynaAC-QV | 0.9 | 0.05 | 0.75 | - |

Table 2: Optimized parameter values.

## 4 Experimental Setup

Our main goal was to evaluate how each algorithm behaves in the following situations:

- The system needs to adapt to a noise free environment.
- The system needs to adapt to a noisy environment.
- There is a change in the environment and the system needs to adapt.

To ensure each algorithm performed to the best of its capabilities we tuned each one's parameters in an exhaustive manner. Table 2 shows the parameter values selected for each algorithm. The parameter $\epsilon$ in $\epsilon$-greedy strategies was set to 0.01 and model-based algorithms trained their model for 15 iterations after each interaction with the environment. Learning rates $\alpha$ and $\beta$ and exploration parameter $\epsilon$ decayed as the episodes progressed to allow better stability.

At each episode the algorithms need enough iterations to explore the state space. At the initial stages of learning, though, it is possible that some algorithms fall into loops and require a very large number of iterations before reaching a terminal state. It would not hurt then if we bound the number of iterations to a reasonable limit, provided it allows enough "negative" rewards to be accumulated when following a "bad" direction. In our evaluation the algorithms were allowed $2|D|$ iterations, ensuring enough steps for exploration but not allowing "bad" directions to be followed for too long.

To assess each algorithm's performance and convergence speed, we run each algorithm 100 times on a slot filling problem with 6 slots, 6 actions and 300 episodes. The average reward over a high number of episodes indicates how stable each algorithm is after convergence. User query $q$ was set to be $\{s_1, ..., s_5\}$ and there was no noise in the environment, meaning that the action of querying a slot deterministically gets the system into a state where that slot is filled. This can be formulated as: $P_t(d_j|d_i, a_m) = 1$, $P_c(s_j) = 1 \forall j$, $\nu = 0$ and $\tilde{A}_{i,j} = 1, \forall i, j$.

To evaluate the algorithms' performance in the presence of uncertainty we run each for 100 times, on the same slot filling problem but with $P_t(d_j|d_i, a_m) \in [1 - \epsilon, 1]$, with varying $\epsilon$ and available action density values. At each run, each algorithm was evaluated using the same transition probabilities and available actions. To assess how the algorithms respond to environmental changes we conducted a similar but noise free experiment, where after a certain number of episodes the query $q$ was changed. Remember that $q$ models the required information for the system to be able to answer with some degree of certainty, so changing $q$ corresponds to requiring different slots to be filled by the user. For this experiment we randomly generated two queries of approximately 65% of the number of slots. The algorithms then needed to learn a policy for the first query and then adapt to the second, when the change occurs. This could, for example, model scenarios where hotel booking becomes unavailable or some airports are closed, in a travel planning ADS. Last, we evaluated each algorithm's scalability, by running each for 100 times on various slot filling problems, beginning with a problem with 4 slots and 4 actions up to a problem with 8 slots and 8 actions. We measured the return averaged over the 100 runs each algorithm achieved.

Despite many notable efforts, a standardized evaluation framework for ADS or DS is still considered an open question by the research community. The work in (Pietquin and Hastie, 2011) provides a very good survey of current techniques that evaluate several aspects of Dialogue Systems. When RL is applied, researchers typically use the reward function as a metric of performance. This will be our evaluation metric as well, since it is common across all algorithms. As defined in section 2.3, it penalizes attempts to answer the user's query with incomplete information as well as lengthy dialogues.

| *Algorithm* | Average Reward |
|---|---|
| SARSA($\lambda$) | -10.5967 |
| LS-SARSA($\lambda$) | -14.3439 |
| Q Learning | -14.8888 |
| Q($\lambda$) | -63.7588 |
| Actor Critic - QV | -15.9245 |
| IAC | -10.5000 |
| NAC | **-5.8273** |
| DynaSARSA($\lambda$) | -11.9758 |
| DynaQ | -14.7270 |
| DynaQ($\lambda$) | -17.1964 |
| DynaAC-QV | -58.4576 |

Table 3: Average Total Reward without noise.

As mentioned earlier in the text we opted for user simulations for our evaluation experiments instead of real users. This method has a number of advantages, for example the fact that we can very quickly generate huge numbers of training examples. One might suggest that since the system is targeted to real users it might not perform as well when trained using simulations. However, as can be seen from our results, there are online algorithms, such as NAC or SARSA($\lambda$), that can adapt well to environmental changes, so it is reasonable to expect such a system to adapt to a real user even if trained using simulations. We can now present the results of our evaluation, as described above and in the next section we will provide insight on the algorithms' behaviour on each experiment.

| *Alg.* | E1 | E2 | E3 | E4 |
|---|---|---|---|---|
| S($\lambda$) | -7.998 | -13.94 | -23.68 | -30.01 |
| LSS | -9.385 | -12.34 | -25.67 | -32.33 |
| Q | -6.492 | -15.71 | -23.36 | -30.56 |
| Q($\lambda$) | -22.44 | -23.27 | -27.04 | -29.37 |
| AC | -8.648 | -17.91 | -32.14 | -38.46 |
| IAC | -6.680 | -18.58 | -33.60 | -35.39 |
| NAC | **-3.090** | **-9.142** | **-19.46** | **-21.33** |
| DS($\lambda$) | -8.108 | -15.61 | -38.22 | -41.90 |
| DQ | -6.390 | -13.04 | -23.64 | -28.69 |
| DQ($\lambda$) | -16.04 | -17.33 | -39.20 | -38.42 |
| DAC | -28.39 | -32.25 | -44.26 | -45.01 |

Table 4: Average Total Reward with noise.

### 4.1 Average reward without noise

Table 3 shows the average total reward each algorithm achieved (i.e. the average of the sum of rewards for each episode), over 100 runs, each run consisting of 300 episodes. The problem had 6 slots, 6 actions, a query $q = \{s_1, ..., s_5\}$ and no noise. In this scenario the algorithms need to learn to request each slot only once and give the answer when all slots are filled. The optimal reward in this case was $-5$. Remember that during the early stages of training the algorithms receive suboptimal rewards until they converge to the optimal policy that yields $J^{\pi^*} = -5$. The sum of rewards an algorithm received for each episode then can give us a rough idea of how quickly it converged and how stable it is. Clearly NAC outperforms all other algorithms with an average reward of $-5.8273$ showing it converges early and is stable from then on. Note that the differences in performance are statistically significant except between LS-SARSA($\lambda$), DynaSARSA($\lambda$) and DynaQ Learning.

### 4.2 Average reward with noise

Table 4 shows results from four similar experiments (E1, E2, E3 and E4), with 4 slots, 4 actions, $q = \{s_1, s_2, s_3\}$ and 100 episodes but in the presence of noise. For E1 we set $P_t(d_j|d_i, a_m) = 1$ and Density to 1, for E2 we set $P_t(d_j|d_i, a_m) = 0.8$ and Density to $0.95$, for E3 we set $P_t(d_j|d_i, a_m) = 0.6$ and Density to $0.9$ and for E4 we set $P_t(d_j|d_i, a_m) = 0.4$ and Density to $0.8$. After each episode we added a small noise $\nu \in [-0.05, 0.05]$ to $P_t(\cdot)$. Remember that each algorithm run for $2|D|$ iterations (32 in this case) for each episode, so an average lower than $-32$ indicates slow convergence or even that the algorithm oscillates. In E1, since there are few slots and no uncertainty, most algorithms, except for IAC, NAC and Q($\lambda$) converge quickly and have statistically insignificant differences with each other. In E2 we have less pairs with statistically insignificant differences, and in E3 and E4 we only have the ones mentioned in the previous section. As we can see, NAC handles uncertainty better, by a considerable margin, than the rest algorithms. Note here that Q($\lambda$) converges late while Q Learning, Dyna Q Learning, SARSA($\lambda$) AC-QV and Dyna SARSA($\lambda$) oscillate a lot in the presence of noise. The optimal reward is $-3$, so it is evident that most algorithms cannot handle uncertainty well.

### 4.3 Response to change

In this experiment we let each algorithm run for 500 episodes in a problem with 6 slots and 6 actions. We generated two queries, $q_1$ and $q_2$, consisting of 4 slots each, and begun the algorithms with $q_1$. After 300 episodes the query was changed to $q_2$ and the algorithms were allowed another 200 episodes to converge. Table 5 shows the episode at which, on average, each algorithm converged after the change (after the $300^{th}$ episode). Note here that the learning rates $\alpha$ and $\beta$ were reset at the point of change. Differences in performance, with respect to the average reward collected during this experiment are statistically significant, except between SARSA($\lambda$), Q Learning and DynaQ($\lambda$). We can see that NAC converges only after 3 episodes on average, with IAC converging after 4. All other algorithms require many more episodes, from about 38 to 134.

| *Algorithm* | Episode |
|---|---|
| SARSA($\lambda$) | 360.5 |
| LS-SARSA($\lambda$) | 337.6 |
| Q Learning | 362.8 |
| Q($\lambda$) | 342.5 |
| Actor Critic - QV | 348.7 |
| IAC | 304.1 |
| NAC | **302.9** |
| DynaSARSA($\lambda$) | 402.6 |
| DynaQ | 380.2 |
| DynaQ($\lambda$) | 384.6 |
| DynaAC-QV | 433.3 |

Table 5: Average number of episodes required for convergence after the change.

### 4.4 Convergence Speed

To assess the algorithms' convergence speed we run each algorithm 100 times for problems of "dimension" 4 to 8 (i.e. 4 slots and 4 actions, 5 slots and 5 actions and so on). We then marked the episode at which each algorithm had converged and averaged it over the 100 runs. Table 6 shows the results. It is important to note here that LS-SARSA, IAC and NAC use function approximation while the rest algorithms do not. We, however, assume that we have enough memory for problems up to 8 slots and 8 actions and are only interested in how many episodes it takes each algorithm to converge, on average. The results show how scalable the algorithms are with respect to computational power.

We can see that after dimension 7 many algorithms require much more episodes in order to converge. LS-SARSA($\lambda$), IAC and NAC once again seem to behave better than the others, requiring only a few more episodes as the problem dimension increases. Note here however that these algorithms take much more absolute time to converge compared to simpler algorithms (eg Q Learning) who might require more episodes but each episode is completed faster.

| *Algorithm* | 4 | 5 | 6 | 7 | 8 |
|---|---|---|---|---|---|
| S($\lambda$) | **5** | 23 | 29 | 42 | 101 |
| LSS($\lambda$) | 10 | 22 | 27 | 38 | 51 |
| Q | 11 | 29 | 47 | 212 | 816 |
| Q($\lambda$) | **5** | 12 | 29 | 55 | 96 |
| AC | 12 | 21 | 42 | 122 | 520 |
| IAC | 7 | 14 | 29 | 32 | 39 |
| NAC | **5** | **9** | **17** | **23** | **28** |
| DS($\lambda$) | **5** | 11 | 22 | 35 | 217 |
| DQ | 15 | 22 | 60 | 186 | 669 |
| DQ($\lambda$) | 9 | 13 | 55 | 72 | 128 |
| DAC | 13 | 32 | 57 | 208 | 738 |

Table 6: Average number of episodes required for convergence on various problem dimensions.

## 5 Discussion

**SARSA($\lambda$)** performed almost equally to IAC at the experiment with deterministic transitions but did not react well to the change in $q$. As we can see in Table 6, SARSA($\lambda$) generally converges at around episode 29 for a problem with 6 slots and 6 actions, therefore the 61 episodes it takes it to adapt to change are somewhat many. This could be due to the fact that SARSA($\lambda$) uses eligibility traces which means that past state - action pairs still contribute to the updates, so even if the learning rate $\alpha$ is reset immediately after the change to allow faster convergence, it seems not enough. It might be possible though to come up with a strategy and deal with this type of situation, for example zero out all traces as well as resetting $\alpha$. SARSA($\lambda$) performs above average in the presence of noise in this particular problem.

**LS-SARSA($\lambda$)** practically is SARSA($\lambda$) with function approximation. While this gives the advantage of requiring less memory, it converges a little slower than SARSA($\lambda$) in the presence of noise or in noise free environments and it needs more episodes to converge as the size of the problem grows. It does, however, react better to changes in the user's goals, since it requires 38 episodes to converge after the change, compared to 27 it normally needs as we can see in Table 6.

**Q Learning** exhibits similar behaviour with the only difference that it converges a little later. Again it takes many episodes to converge after the change in the environment (compared to the 47 that it needs initially). This could be explained by the fact that Q Learning only updates one row of $Q(x, a)$ at each iteration, thus needing more iterations for $Q(x, a)$ to reflect expected rewards in the new environment. Like SARSA($\lambda$), Q Learning is able to deal with uncertainty well enough on the dialogue task in the given time, but does not scale well.

**Q($\lambda$)** , quite opposite from SARSA($\lambda$) and Q Learning, is the slowest to initially converge, but handles changes in the environment much better. In Q($\lambda$) the update of $Q(x, a)$ is (very roughly) based on the difference of $Q(x, a') - Q(x, a^*)$ where $a^*$ is the best possible action the algorithm can take, whereas in SARSA($\lambda$) the update is (again roughly) based on $Q(x, a') - Q(x, a)$. Also, in Q($\lambda$) eligibility traces become zero if the selected action is not the best possible. These two reasons help obsolete information in $Q(x, a)$ be quickly updated. While it performs worse in the presence of uncertainty, the average reward does not drop as steeply as for the rest algorithms.

**AC-QV** converges better than average, compared to the other algorithms, and seems to cope well with changes in the environment. While it needs 42 episodes, on average, to converge for a problem of 6 slots and 6 actions, it only needs around 49 episodes to converge again after a change. Unlike SARSA($\lambda$) and Q($\lambda$) it does not have eligibility traces to delay the update of $Q(x, a)$ (or $P(x, a)$ for Preferences in this case, see (Wiering and Van Hasselt, 2009)) while it also keeps track of $V(x)$. The updates are then based on the difference of $P(x, a)$ and $V(x)$ which, from our results, seems to make this algorithm behave better in a dynamic environment. AC-QV also cannot cope with uncertainty very well on this problem.

**IAC** is an actor - critic algorithm that follows the gradient of cumulative discounted rewards $\nabla J^{\pi}$. It always performs slightly worse than NAC but in a consistent way, except in the experiments with noise. It only requires approximately 4 episodes to converge after a change but cannot handle noise as well as other algorithms. This can be in part explained by the policy gradient theorem (Sutton et al., 2000) according to which changes in the policy do not affect the distribution of state the system visits (IAC and NAC perform gradient ascend in the space of policies rather than in parameter space (Szepesvári, 2010)). Policy gradient methods in general seem to converge rapidly, as supported by results of Sutton et al. (2000) or Konda and Tsitsiklis (2001) for example.

**NAC** , as expected, performs better than any other algorithm in all settings. It not only converges in very few episodes but is also very robust to noise and changes in the environment. Following the natural gradient has proven to be much more efficient than simply using the gradient of the expected rewards. There are many positive examples of NAC performance (or following the natural gradient in general), such as (Bagnell and Schneider, 2003; Peters et al., 2005) and this work is one of them.

**Dyna Algorithms** except for Dyna SARSA($\lambda$), seem to perform worse than average on the deterministic problem. In the presence of changes, none of them seems to perform very well. These algorithms use a model of the environment to update $Q(x,a)$ or $P(x,a)$, meaning that after each interaction with the environment they perform several iterations using simulated triplets $(x,a,r)$. In the presence of changes this results in obsolete information being reused again and again until sufficient real interactions with the environment occur and the model is updated as well. This is possibly the main reason why each Dyna algorithm requires more episodes after the change than its corresponding learning algorithm. Dyna Q Learning only updates a single entry of $Q(x,a)$ at each simulated iteration, which could explain why noise does not corrupt $Q(x,a)$ too much and why this algorithm performs well in the presence of uncertainty. Noise in this case is added at a single entry of $Q(x,a)$, rather than to the whole matrix, at each iteration. Dyna SARSA($\lambda$) and Dyna Q($\lambda$) handle noise slightly better than Dyna AC-QV.

## 6 Concluding Remarks

NAC proved to be the best algorithm in our evaluation. It is, however, much more complex to implement and run and thus each episode takes more (absolute) time to complete. One might suggest then that a lighter algorithm such as SARSA($\lambda$) will have the opportunity to run more iterations in the same absolute time. One should definitely take this into account when designing a real world system, when timely responses are necessary and resources are limited as, for example, in a mobile system. Note that SARSA($\lambda$), Q-Learning, Q($\lambda$) and AC-QV are significantly faster than the rest algorithms.

On the other hand, all algorithms except for NAC, IAC and LS-SARSA have the major drawback of the size of the table representing $Q(x,a)$ or $P(x,a)$ that is needed to store state-action values. This is a disadvantage that practically prohibits the use of these algorithms in high dimensional or continuous problems. Function approximation might alleviate this problem, according to Bertsekas (2007), if we reformulate the problem and reduce control space while increasing state space. In such a setting function approximation performs well, while in general it cannot deal with large control spaces. It becomes very expensive as computation cost grows exponentially on the size of the lookahead horizon. Also, according to Sutton and Barto (1998) and Sutton et al. (2000), better convergence guarantees exist for online algorithms when combined with function approximation or for policy gradient methods (such as IAC or NAC) in general. Finally, one must take great care when selecting features to approximate $Q(x,a)$ or $V(x)$ as they are important to convergence and speed of the algorithm (Allen and Fritzsche, 2011; Bertsekas, 2007).

To summarize, NAC outperforms the other algorithms in every experiment we conducted. It does require a lot of computational power though and might not be suitable if it is limited. On the other hand, SARSA($\lambda$) or Q Learning perform well enough while requiring less computational power but a lot more memory space. The researcher / developer then must make his / her choice between them taking into account such practical limitations.

As future work we plan to implement these algorithms on the Olympus / RavenClaw (Bohus and Rudnicky, 2009) platform, using the results of this work as a guide. Our aim will be to create a hybrid state of the art ADS that will combine advantages of existing state of the art techniques. Moreover we plan to install our system on a robotic platform and conduct real user trials.

## References


Allen, M., Fritzsche, P., 2011, *Reinforcement Learning with Adaptive Kanerva Encoding for Xpilot Game AI*, Annual Congress on Evolutionary Computation, pp 1521–1528.

Atkeson, C.G., Santamaria, J.C., 1997, *A comparison of direct and model-based reinforcement learning*, IEEE Robotics and Automation, pp 3557–3564.

Bagnell, J., Schneider, J., 2003, *Covariant policy search*, Proceedings of the Eighteenth International Joint Conference on Artificial Intelligence, pp 1019–1024.

Bertsekas D.P., 2007, *Dynamic Programming and Optimal Control*, Athena Scientific, vol 2, 3rd edition.

Bhatnagar, S, Sutton, R.S., Ghavamzadeh, M., Lee, M. 2007, *Incremental Natural Actor-Critic Algorithms*, Neural Information Processing Systems, pp 105–112.

Bohus, D., Rudnicky, A.I., 2009, *The RavenClaw dialog management framework: Architecture and systems*, Computer Speech & Language, vol 23:3, pp 332-361.

Boidin, C., Rieser, V., Van Der Plas, L., Lemon, O., and Chevelu, J. 2009, *Predicting how it sounds: Re-ranking dialogue prompts based on TTS quality for adaptive Spoken Dialogue Systems*, Proceedings of the Interspeech Special Session Machine Learning for Adaptivity in Spoken Dialogue, pp 2487–2490.

Chen, S-L., Wei, Y-M. 2008, *Least-Squares SARSA(Lambda) Algorithms for Reinforcement Learning*, Natural Computation, 2008. ICNC '08, vol.2, pp 632–636.

Cuayáhuitl, H., Renals, S., Lemon, O., Shimodaira, H. 2010, *Evaluation of a hierarchical reinforcement learning spoken dialogue system*, Computer Speech & Language, Academic Press Ltd., vol 24:2, pp 395–429.

Gašić, M., Jurčíček, F., Keizer, S., Mairesse, F. and Thomson, B., Yu, K. and Young, S, 2010, *Gaussian processes for fast policy optimisation of POMDP-based dialogue managers*, Proceedings of the 11th Annual Meeting of the Special Interest Group on Discourse and Dialogue, pp 201–204.

Geist, M., Pietquin, O., 2010, *Kalman temporal differences*, Journal of Artificial Intelligence Research, vol 39:1, pp 483–532.

Janarthanam, S., Lemon, O. 2009, *A Two-Tier User Simulation Model for Reinforcement Learning of Adaptive Referring Expression Generation Policies*, SIGDIAL Conference'09, pp 120–123.

Jurčíček, F., Thomson, B., Keizer, S., Mairesse, F., Gašić, M., Yu, K., Young, S 2010, *Natural Belief-Critic: A Reinforcement Algorithm for Parameter Estimation in Statistical Spoken Dialogue Systems*, International Speech Communication Association, vol 7, pp 1–26.

Konda, V.R., Tsitsiklis, J.N., 2001, *Actor-Critic Algorithms*, SIAM Journal on Control and Optimization, MIT Press, pp 1008–1014.

Konstantopoulos S., 2010, *An Embodied Dialogue System with Personality and Emotions*, Proceedings of the 2010 Workshop on Companionable Dialogue Systems, ACL 2010, pp 3136.

Papangelis, A., Karkaletsis, V., Makedon, F., 2012, *Evaluation of Online Dialogue Policy Learning Techniques*, Proceedings of the 8th Conference on Language Resources and Evaluation (LREC) 2012, to appear.

Peng, J., Williams, R., 1996, *Incremental multi-step Q-Learning*, Machine Learning pp 283–290.

Peters, J., Vijayakumar, S., Schaal, S. 2005, *Natural actor-critic* , Machine Learning: ECML 2005, pp 280–291.

Pietquin, O., Hastie H. 2011, *A survey on metrics for the evaluation of user simulations*, The Knowledge Engineering Review, Cambridge University Press (to appear).

Rieser, V., Lemon, O. 2009, *Natural Language Generation as Planning Under Uncertainty for Spoken Dialogue Systems*, Proceedings of the 12th Conference of the European Chapter of the ACL (EACL 2009), pp 683–691.

Ross, S., Pineau, J., Paquet, S., Chaib-draa, B., 2008, *Online planning algorithms for POMDPs*, Journal of Artificial Intelligence Research, pp 663–704.

Sutton R.S., Barto, A.G., 1998, *Reinforcement Learning: An Introduction*, The MIT Press, Cambridge, MA.

Sutton, R.S.,Mcallester, D., Singh, S., Mansour, Y. 2000, *Policy gradient methods for reinforcement learning with function approximation*, In Advances in Neural Information Processing Systems 12, pp 1057–1063.

Szepesvári, C., 2010, *Algorithms for Reinforcement Learning*, Morgan & Claypool Publishers, Synthesis Lectures on Artificial Intelligence and Machine Learning, vol 4:1, pp 1–103.

Watkins C.J.C.H., 1989, *Learning from delayed rewards*, PhD Thesis, University of Cambridge, England.

Wiering, M. A, Van Hasselt, H. 2009, *The QV family compared to other reinforcement learning algorithms*, IEEE Symposium on Adaptive Dynamic Programming and Reinforcement Learning, pp 101–108.

Young S., Gašić, M., Keizer S., Mairesse, F., Schatzmann J., Thomson, B., Yu, K., 2010, *The Hidden Information State model: A practical framework for POMDP-based spoken dialogue management*, Computer Speech & Language, vol 24:2, pp 150–174.

# Manually Constructed Context-Free Grammar For Myanmar Syllable Structure

**Tin Htay Hlaing**
Nagaoka University of Technology
Nagaoka, JAPAN
tinhtayhlaing@gmail.com

## Abstract

Myanmar language and script are unique and complex. Up to our knowledge, considerable amount of work has not yet been done in describing Myanmar script using formal language theory. This paper presents manually constructed context free grammar (CFG) with "111" productions to describe the Myanmar Syllable Structure. We make our CFG in conformity with the properties of LL(1) grammar so that we can apply conventional parsing technique called predictive top-down parsing to identify Myanmar syllables. We present Myanmar syllable structure according to orthographic rules. We also discuss the preprocessing step called contraction for vowels and consonant conjuncts. We make LL (1) grammar in which "1" does not mean exactly one character of lookahead for parsing because of the above mentioned contracted forms. We use five basic sub syllabic elements to construct CFG and found that all possible syllable combinations in Myanmar Orthography can be parsed correctly using the proposed grammar.

## 1 Introduction

Formal Language Theory is a common way to represent grammatical structures of natural languages and programming languages. The origin of grammar hierarchy is the pioneering work of Noam Chomsky (Noam Chomsky, 1957). A huge amount of work has been done in Natural Language Processing where Chomsky`s grammar is used to describe the grammatical rules of natural languages. However, formulation rules have not been established for grammar for Myanmar script. The long term goal of this study is to develop automatic syllabification of Myanmar polysyllabic words using regular grammar and/or finite state methods so that syllabified strings can be used for Myanmar sorting.

In this paper, as a preliminary stage, we describe the structure of a Myanmar syllable in context-free grammar and parse the syllables using predictive top-down parsing technique to determine whether a given syllable can be recognized by the proposed grammar or not. Further, the constructed grammar includes linguistic information and follows the traditional writing system of Myanmar script.

## 2 Myanmar Script

Myanmar is a syllabic script and also one of the languages which have complex orthographic structures. Myanmar words are formed by collection of syllables and each syllable may contain up to seven different sub syllabic elements. Again, each component group has its own members having specific order.

Basically, Myanmar script has 33 consonants, 8 vowels (free standing and attached)[1] , 2 diacritics, 11 medials, a vowel killer or ASAT, 10 digits and 2 punctuation marks.

A Myanmar syllable consists of 7 different components in Backus Normal Form (BNF) is as follows.

S:= C{M}{V}[CK][D] | I[CK] | N

where

S = Syllable

1. C = Consonant
2. M = Medial or Consonant Conjunct or attached consonant

[1] Free standing vowel syllables (eg. ဣ )and attached vowel symbols (eg. ု )

3. V = Attached Vowel
4. K = Vowel Killer or ASAT
5. D = Diacritic
6. I = Free standing Vowel
7. N = Digit

And the notation [ ] means 0 or 1 occurrence and { } means 0 or more occurrence.
However, in this paper, we ignore digits, free standing vowel and punctuation marks in writing grammar for Myanmar syllable and we focus only on basic and major five sub syllabic groups namely consonants(C), medial(M), attached vowels(V), a vowel killer (K) and diacritics(D). The following subsection will give the details of each sub syllabic group.

### 2.1 Brief Description of Basic Myanmar Sub Syllabic Elements

Each Myanmar consonant has default vowel sound and itself works as a syllable. The set of consonants in Unicode chart is C={က, ခ, ဂ, ဃ, င, စ, ဆ, ဇ, ဈ, ဉ , ည ,ဋ ,ဌ, ဍ, ဎ, ဏ, တ, ထ ,ဒ ,ဓ ,န ,ပ ,ဖ, ဗ, ဘ ,မ ,ယ ,ရ, လ, ဝ, သ, ဟ, ဠ } having 33 elements. But, the letter အ can act as consonant as well as free standing vowel.

Medials or consonant conjuncts mean the modifiers of the syllables` vowel and they are encoded separately in the Unicode encoding. There are four basic medials in Unicode chart and it is represented as the set M={◌ျ, ◌ြ, ◌ွ, ◌ှ}.

The set V of Myanmar attached vowel characters in Unicode contains 8 elements { ◌ါ, ◌ာ, ◌ိ, ◌ီ, ◌ု, ◌ူ, ◌ေ, ◌ဲ}. ( Peter and William, 1996)

Diacritics alter the vowel sounds of accompanying consonants and they are used to indicate tone level. There are 2 diacritical marks { ◌့, ◌း } in Myanmar script and the set is represented as D.

The asat, or killer, representing the set K= { ◌် } is a visibly displayed sign. In some cases it indicates that the inherent vowel sound of a consonant letter is suppressed. In other cases it combines with other characters to form a vowel letter. Regardless of its function, this visible sign is always represented by the character U+103A .[2] [John Okell, 1994]

In Unicode chart, the diacritics group D and the vowel killer or ASAT "K" are included in the group named various signs.

### 2.2 Preprocessing of Texts - Contraction

In writing formal grammar for a Myanmar syllable, there are some cases where two or more Myanmar characters combine each other and the resulting combined forms are also used in Myanmar traditional writing system though they are not coded directly in the Myanmar Unicode chart. Such combinations of vowel and medials are described in detail below.
Two or more Myanmar attached vowels are combined and formed new three members { ◌ော, ◌ော်, ◌ို } in the vowel set.

| Glyph | Unicode for Contraction | Description |
|---|---|---|
| ◌ေ + ◌ာ | 1031+102C | Vowel sign E + AA |
| ◌ေ + ◌ာ + ◌် | 1031+102C+103A | Vowel sign E +AA+ASAT |
| ◌ိ + ◌ု | 102D + 102F | Vowel sign I + UU |

"Table 1. Contractions of vowels"

Similarly, 4 basic Myanmar medials combine each other in some different ways and produce new set of medials { ◌ျွ, ◌ြွ, ◌ျှ, ◌ြှ, ◌ွှ, ◌ျွှ , ◌ြွှ }. [Tin Htay Hlaing and Yoshiki Mikami, 2011]

| Glyph | Unicode for Contraction | Description |
|---|---|---|
| ◌ျ + ◌ွ | 103B + 103D | Consonant Sign Medial YA + WA |
| ◌ြ + ◌ွ | 103C + 103D | Consonant Sign Medial RA + WA |
| ◌ျ + ◌ှ | 103B + 103E | Consonant Sign Medial YA + HA |
| ◌ြ + ◌ှ | 103C + 103E | Consonant Sign Medial RA + HA |

[2] http://www.unicode.org/versions/Unicode6.0.0/ch11.pdf

| | | |
|---|---|---|
| ွ + ှ | 103D + 103E | Consonant Sign Medial WA + HA |
| ျ + ွ + ှ | 103B + 103D + 103E | Consonant Sign Medial YA+WA + HA |
| ြ + ွ + ှ | 103C + 103D + 103E | Consonant Sign Medial YA+WA + HA |

"Table 2. Contractions of Medials"

The above mentioned combinations of characters are considered as one vowel or medial in constructing the grammar. The complete sets of elements for vowels and meidals used in writing grammar are depicted in the table below.[3]

| Name of Sub Syllabic Component | Elements |
|---|---|
| Medials or Conjunct Consonants | ျ, ြ, ွ, ှ, ျွ, ြွ, ျှ, ြှ, ွှ, ျွှ, ြွှ |
| Attached vowels | ါ, ာ, ိ, ီ, ု, ူ, ေ, ဲ, ော, ော်, ံ, ို |

"Table 3. List of vowels and Medials"

## 2.3 Combinations of Syllabic Components within a Syllable

As mentioned in the earlier sections, we choose only 5 basic sub syllabic components namely consonants (C), medial (M), attached vowels (V), vowel killer (K) and diacritics (D) to describe Myanmar syllable. As our intended use for syllabification is for sorting, we omit stand-alone vowels and digits in describing Myanmar syllable structure. Further, according to the sorting order of Myanmar Orthography, stand-alone vowels are sorted as the syllable using the above 5 sub syllabic elements having the same pronunciation. For example, stand-alone vowel "ဣ" is sorted as consonant "အ" and attached vowel "ိ" combination as "အိ".

[3] Sorting order of Medials and attached vowels in Myanmar Orthography

In Myanmar language, *a syllable with only one consonant can be taken as one syllable* because Myanmar script is Abugida which means all letters have inherent vowel. And, consonants can be followed by vowels, consonant, vowel killer and medials in different combinations.

One special feature is that if there are two consonants in a given syllable, the second consonant must be followed by vowel killer (K). We found that 1872 combinations of sub-syllabic elements in Myanmar Orthography [Myanmar Language Commission, 2006]. The table below shows top level combinations of these sub-syllabic elements.

| **Consonant only** | **Consonant followed by Vowel** | **Consonant followed by Consonant** | **Consonant followed by Medial** |
|---|---|---|---|
| C | CV<br>CVCK<br>CVD<br>CVCKD | CCK<br>CCKD | CM<br>CMV<br>CMVD<br>CMVCK<br>CMVCKD<br>CMCK<br>CMCKD |

"Table 4. Possible Combinations within a Syllable"

The combinations among five basic sub syllabic components can also be described using Finite State Automaton. We also find that Myanmar orthographic syllable structure can be described in regular grammar.

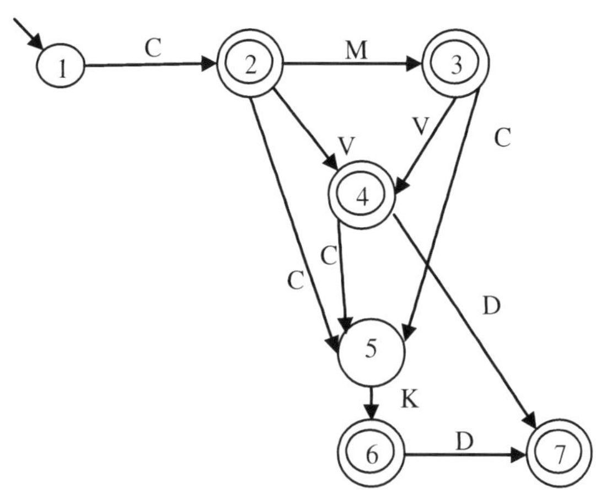


"Figure 1. FSA for a Myanmar Syllable"

In the above FSA, an interesting point is that only one consonant can be a syllable because Myanmar consonants have default vowel sounds. That is why, state 2 can be a final state. For instance, a Myanmar Word "မိန်းမ" (means "Woman" in English) has two syllables. In the first syllable "မိန်း", the sub syllabic elements are Consonant(မ) + Vowel(ိ) +Consonant(န)+ Vowel Killer(်)+Diacritics(း). The second syllable has only one consonant "မ".

## 3 Myanmar Syllable Structure in Context-Free Grammar

### 3.1 Manually Constructed Context-Free Grammar for Myanmar Syllable Structure

Context free (CF) grammar refers to the grammar rules of languages which are formulated independently of any context. A CF-grammar is defined by:

1. A finite terminal vocabulary $V_T$.
2. A finite auxiliary vocabulary $V_A$.
3. An axiom $S \in V_A$.
4. A finite number of context-free rules P of the form $A \rightarrow \phi$ where

$A \in V_A$ and $\phi \in \{V_A \cup V_T\}^*$ (M.Gross and A.Lentin, 1970)

The grammar G to represent all possible structures of a Myanmar syllable can be written as $G=(V_T, V_A, P, S)$ where the elements of P are:

S→က X

# Such production will be expanded for 33 consonants.

X→ ျA

# Such production will be expanded for 11 medials.

X→ ာB

# Such production will be expanded for 12 vowels.

X→C ် D

X→ε

A→ ာ B

# Such production will be expanded for 12 vowels.

A→ C ် D

A→ε

B → C ် D

B→ D

B→ε

D→ း # Diacritics

D→ ံ # Diacritics

D→ ε

C→ က

# Such production will be expanded for 33 consonants.

Total number of productions/rules to recognize Myanmar syllable structure is "111" and we found that the director symbol sets (which is also known as first and follow sets) for same non-terminal symbols with different productions are disjoint.

This is the property of LL(1) grammar which means for each non terminal that appears on the left side of more than one production, the directory symbol sets of all the productions in which it appears on the left side are disjoint. Therefore, our proposed grammar can be said as LL(1) grammar.

The term LL1 is made up as follows. The first L means reading from Left to right, the second L means using Leftmost derivations, and the "1" means with one symbol of lookahead. (Robin Hunter, 1999)

### 3.2 Parse Table for Myanmar CFG

The following figure is a part of parse table made from the productions of the proposed LL(1) grammar.

| | က | င | ျ | ာ | း | ံ | ် | $ |
|---|---|---|---|---|---|---|---|---|
| S | S→ကX | S→င X | | | | | | |
| X | X→C ် D | X →C ် D | X → ျ A | X → ာ B | | | | X →ε |
| A | A→C ် D | A →C ် D | | A → ာ B | | | | A →ε |
| B | B→C ် D | B→C ် D | | | B→D | B→D | | B →ε |
| D | | | | | D → း | D →ံ | | D →ε |
| C | C→က | C→င | | | | | | |

"Table 5. Parse Table for Myanmar Syllable"

In the above table, the topmost row represents terminal symbols whereas the leftmost column represents the non terminal symbols. The entries in the table are productions to apply for each pair of non terminal and terminal.

An example of Myanmar syllable having 4 different sub syllabic elements is parsed using proposed grammar and the above parse table. The parsing steps show proper working of the proposed grammar and the detail of parsing a syllable is as follows.

Input Syllable = ကျား =က(C) + ◌ျ(M)+ ◌ာ (V)+◌း (D)

| Parse Stack | Remaining Input | Parser Action |
|---|---|---|
| S $ | က ◌ျ ◌ာ း $ | S→ကX |
| ကX $ | က ◌ျ ◌ာ း $ | MATCH |
| ~~က~~ X $ | ~~က~~ ◌ျ ◌ာ း $ | X→ ◌ျA |
| ~~က~~ ◌ျA $ | ~~က~~ ◌ျ ◌ာ း $ | MATCH |
| ~~က~~ ~~◌ျ~~A $ | ~~က~~ ~~◌ျ~~ ◌ာ း $ | A→ ◌ာB |
| ~~က~~ ~~◌ျ~~ ◌ာ B $ | ~~က~~ ~~◌ျ~~ ◌ာ း $ | MATCH |
| ~~က~~ ~~◌ျ~~ ~~◌ာ~~B $ | ~~က~~ ~~◌ျ~~ ~~◌ာ~~ း $ | B→D |
| ~~က~~ ~~◌ျ~~ ~~◌ာ~~ D $ | ~~က~~ ~~◌ျ~~ ~~◌ာ~~ း $ | D→ း |
| ~~က~~ ~~◌ျ~~ ~~◌ာ~~ -း $ | ~~က~~ ~~◌ျ~~ ~~◌ာ~~ း $ | MATCH |
| ~~က~~ ~~◌ျ~~ ~~◌ာ~~ ~~း~~ $ | ~~း~~ $ | SUCCESS |

"Table 6. Parsing a Myanmar Syllable using predictive top-down parsing method"

## 4 Conclusion

This study shows the powerfulness of Chomsky`s context free grammar as it can apply not only to describe the sentence structure but also the syllable structure of an Asian script, Myanmar. Though the number of productions in the proposed grammar for Myanmar syllable is large, the syntactic structure of a Myanmar syllable is correctly recognized and the grammar is not ambiguous.

Further, in parsing Myanmar syllable, it is necessary to do preprocessing called contraction for input sequences of vowels and consonant conjuncts or medials to meet the requirements of traditional writing systems. However, because of these contracted forms, single lookahead symbol in our proposed LL(1) grammar does not refer exactly to one character and it may be a combination of two or more characters in parsing Myanmar syllable.

## 5 Discussion and Future Work

Myanmar script is syllabic as well as aggulutinative script. Every Myanmar word or sentence is composed of series of individual syllables. Thus, it is critical to have efficient way of recognizing syllables in conformity with the rules of Myanmar traditional writing system.

Our intended research is the automatic syllabification of Myanmar polysyllabic words using formal language theory.

One option to do is to modify our current CFG to recognize consecutive syllables as a first step. We found that if the current CFG is changed for sequence of syllables, the grammar can be no longer LL(1). Then, we need to use one of the statistical methods, for example, probabilistic CFG, to choose correct productions or best parse for finding syllable boundaries.

Again, it is necessary to calculate the probability values for each production based on the frequency of occurrence of a syllable in a dictionary we referred or using TreeBank.

We need Myanmar corpus or a tree bank which contains evidence for rule expansions for syllable structure and such a resource does not yet exist for Myanmar. And also, the time and cost for constructing a corpus by ourselves came into consideration.

Another approach is to construct finite state transducer for automatic syllabification of Myanmar words. If we choose this approach, we firstly need to construct regular grammar to recognize Myanmar syllables. We already have Myanmar syllable structure in regular grammar. However, for finite state syllabification using weights, there is a lack of resource for training database.

We still have many language specific issues to be addressed for implementing Myanmar script using CFG or FSA. As a first issue, our current grammar is based on five basic sub-syllabic elements and thus developing the grammar which can handle all seven Myanmar sub syllabic elements will be future study.

Our current grammar is based on the code point values of the input syllables or words. Then, as a second issue, we need to consider about different presentations or code point values of same character. Moreover, we have special writing traditions for some characters, for example, such as consonant stacking eg. ဗုဒ္ဓ (Buddha), မန္တလေး (Mandalay, second capital of Myanmar), consonant repetition eg. တက္ကသိုလ် (University), kinzi eg. အင်္ဂတေ (Cement), loan words eg. ဘတ်(စ်) (bus). To represent such complex forms in a computer system, we use invisible Virama sign (U+1039). Therefore, it is necessary to construct the productions which have conformity with the stored character code sequence of Myanmar Language.

## References


John Okell. " Burmese An Introduction to the Script". Northern Illinois University Press, 1994.

M.Gross, A.Lentin. "Introduction to Formal Grammar". Springer-Verlag, 1970.

Myanmar Language Commission. *Myanmar Orthography,* Third Edition, University Press, Yangon, Myanmar, 2006.

Noam Chomsky. "Syntactic Structures". Mouton De Gruyter, Berlin, 1957.

Peter T. Denials, William Bright. "World`s Writing System". Oxford University Press, 1996.

Robin Hunter. "The Essence of Compilers". Prentice Hall, 1999.

Tin Htay Hlaing, Yoshiki Mikami. " Collation Weight Design for Myanmar Unicode Texts" in Proceedings of Human Language Technology for Development organized by PAN Localization- Asia, AnLoc – Africa, IDRC – Canada. May 2011, Alexandria, EGYPT, Page 1- 6.

# What's in a Name?
# Entity Type Variation across Two Biomedical Subdomains

**Claudiu Mihăilă and Riza Theresa Batista-Navarro**
National Centre for Text Mining
School of Computer Science, University of Manchester
Manchester Interdisciplinary Biocentre,
131 Princess Street, M1 7DN, Manchester, UK
claudiu.mihaila@cs.man.ac.uk
riza.batista-navarro@cs.man.ac.uk

## Abstract

There are lexical, syntactic, semantic and discourse variations amongst the languages used in various biomedical subdomains. It is important to recognise such differences and understand that biomedical tools that work well on some subdomains may not work as well on others. We report here on the semantic variations that occur in the sublanguages of two biomedical subdomains, i.e. cell biology and pharmacology, at the level of named entity information. By building a classifier using ratios of named entities as features, we show that named entity information can discriminate between documents from each subdomain. More specifically, our classifier can distinguish between documents belonging to each subdomain with an accuracy of 91.1% F-score.

## 1 Introduction

Biomedical information extraction efforts in the past decade have focussed on fundamental tasks needed to create intelligent systems capable of improving search engine results and easing the work of biologists. More specifically, researchers have concentrated mainly on named entity recognition, mapping them to concepts in curated databases (Krallinger et al., 2008) and extracting simple binary relations between entities. Recently, an increasing number of resources that facilitate the training of systems to extract more detailed information have become available, e.g., PennBioIE (Kulick et al., 2004), GENETAG (Tanabe et al., 2005), BioInfer (Pyysalo et al., 2007), GENIA (Kim et al., 2008), GREC (Thompson et al., 2009) and Metaknowledge GENIA (Thompson et al., 2011). Moreover, several other annotated corpora have been developed for shared task purposes, such as BioCreative I, II, III (Arighi et al., 2011) and BioNLP Shared Tasks 2009 and 2011 (Cohen et al., 2009; Kim et al., 2011).

Many of the tools currently used for biomedical language processing were trained and evaluated on such popular corpora, most of which consist of documents from the molecular biology subdomain. However, previous studies (discussed in Section 2) have established that different biomedical sublanguages exhibit linguistic variations. It follows that tools which were developed and evaluated on corpora derived from one subdomain might not always perform as well on corpora from other subdomains. Understanding these linguistic variations is essential to the process of adaptating natural language processing tools to new domains.

In this paper, we highlight the variations between biomedical sublanguages by focussing on the different types of named entities (NEs) that are relevant to them. We show that the frequencies of different named entity types vary enough to allow a classifier for scientific subdomains to be built based upon them.

The study is performed on open access journal articles present in the UK PubMed Central[1] (UKPMC) (McEntyre et al., 2010), an article database that extends the functionality of the original PubMed Central (PMC) repository[2]. This database was chosen as our source, since most of the documents within it are already tagged with named entity information. We report here on the results obtained for two biomedical subdomains,

[1]http://ukpmc.ac.uk/

[2]http://www.ncbi.nlm.nih.gov/pmc

i.e. cell biology and pharmacology. Our focus on these two particular subdomains is motivated by an increasing interest expressed by the biomedical research community, according to recent findings that have shown their relevance to discovering possible causes and treatments for incurable diseases, such as cancer or Alzheimer's Disease.

## 2 Related work

Harris (1968) introduced a formalisation of the notion of sublanguage, which was defined as a subset of general language. According to this theory, it is possible to process specialised languages, since they have a structure that can be expressed in a computable form. More recently, several works on the study of biomedical languages substantiated his theory.

For instance, Sager et al. (1987) worked on pharmacological literature and lipid metabolism, whereas Friedman et al. (2002) analysed the properties of clinical and biomolecular sublanguages.

Other studies have investigated the differences between general and biomedical languages by focussing on specific linguistic aspects, such as verb-argument relations and pronominal anaphora. For instance, Wattarujeekrit et al. (2004) analysed the predicate-argument structures of 30 verbs used in biomedical articles. Their results suggest that, in certain cases, a significant difference exists in the predicate frames compared to those obtained from analysing news articles in the PropBank project (Palmer et al., 2005). Similarly, based on the GENIA and PennBioIE corpora, Cohen et al. (2008) performed a study of argument realisation with respect to the nominalisation and alternation of biomedical verbs. They concluded that there is a high occurrence of these phenomena in this semantically restricted domain, and underline that this sublanguage model applies only to biomedical language.

Taking a different angle, Nguyen and Kim (2008) examined the differences in the use of pronouns by studying general domains (MUC and ACE) and one biomedical domain (GENIA). They observed that compared to the MUC and ACE corpora, the GENIA corpus has significantly more occurrences of neutral and third-person pronouns, whilst first and second person pronouns are non-existent.

Verspoor et al. (2009) measured lexical and structural variation in biomedical Open Access journals and subscription-based journals, concluding that there are no significant differences between them. Therefore, a model trained on one of these sources can be used successfully on the other, as long as the subject matter is maintained. Furthermore, they compared a mouse genomics corpus with two reference corpora, one composed of newswire texts and another of general biomedical articles. In this case, unsurprisingly, significant differences were found across many linguistic dimensions. Relevant to our study is the comparison between the more specific mouse genome corpus to the more general biomedical one: whilst similar from some points of view, such as negation and passivisation, they differ in sentence length and semantic features, such as the presence of various named entities.

Our work is most similar to that of Lippincott et al. (2011), in which a clustering-based quantitative analysis of the linguistic variations across 38 different biomedical sublanguages is presented. They investigated four dimensions relevant to the performance of NLP systems, i.e. vocabulary, syntax, semantics and discourse structure. With regard to semantic features, the authors induced a topic model using Latent Dirichlet Analysis for each word, and then extended the model to documents and subdomains according to observed distributions. Their conclusion is that a machine learning system is able to create robust clusters of subdomains, thus proving their hypothesis that the commonly used molecular biology subdomain is not representative of the domain as a whole.

In contrast, we examine the differences between biomedical sublanguages at the semantic level, using only named entities. Furthermore, we choose to perform our analysis only on two subdomains (i.e. cell biology and pharmacology), and try to classify these by using supervised machine learning algorithms.

## 3 Methodology

We designed an experiment in which various machine learning algorithms are trained and tested on data obtained from open access journal articles. Firstly, a corpus of articles was created (Section 3.1), after which the documents were automatically annotated with named entities (Section 3.2). We then extracted a number features relevant to the named entities present in the corpus (Section 3.3).

### 3.1 Corpus development

Our corpus was created by first searching the NLM Catalog[3] for journals whose Broad Subject Term attributes contain only *cell biology* or *pharmacology*, and then narrowing down the results to those which are in English and available via PubMed Central. Also, since we are concentrating on full-text documents, we retained only those journals that are available within the PubMed Open Access subset[4]. According to this procedure, we obtained a final list of two journals for cell biology and six for pharmacology.

Using the PMC IDs of all articles published in the selected journals, we retrieved documents from UK PubMed Central. This database was chosen as our source as the documents it contains are already tagged with named entity information. A total of 360 articles was retrieved for each category, i.e. cell biology and pharmacology.

The retrieved documents were encoded in XML format. Several unusable fragments were removed before converting them to plain text. Examples of such fragments are article metadata (authors, their affiliations, publishing history, etc.), tables, figures and references. Table 1 shows the statistics regarding the corpus following the application of the pre-processing step. In the case of pharmacology, the document collection contains almost 1.4 million words, whilst the set of cell biology articles consists of almost 2.5 million words. The ratio of named entities to the total number of words is almost the same in the two collections, i.e. about 10%.

| Subdomain | Cell biology | Pharmacology |
|---|---|---|
| No. of docs. | 360 | 360 |
| No. of words | 2.49 m. | 1.35 m. |
| No. of NEs | 231761 | 103484 |

Table 1: Named entity types and their source.

### 3.2 Tagging of Named Entities

To extract named entities from the corpus, we used a simple method that augments the named entities present in the UKPMC articles with the output of two named entity recognition tools (NERs), i.e. NeMine and OSCAR. The types of entities in the output be each of the two tools, together with the NE types present in the UKPMC articles, are summarised in Table 2.

Named entities in the UKPMC database were identified using NeMine (Sasaki et al., 2008), a dictionary-based statistical named entity recognition system. This system was later extended and used by Nobata et al. (2009) to recognise more types, such as phenomena, processes, organs and symptoms. We used this most recent version of the software as our second source of more diverse entity types.

The Open-Source Chemistry Analysis Routines (OSCAR) software (Jessop et al., 2011) is a toolkit for the recognition of named entities and data in chemistry publications. Currently in its fourth version, it uses three types of chemical entity recognisers, namely regular expressions, patterns and Maximum Entropy Markov models.

In total, 20 different classes of entities were considered in this study. However, due to the combination of several NERs, some NE types are identified by more than one NER. Furthermore, some of the NE types are more general and cover other more specific types, which are also annotated by one or mroe of the tools. This can lead to double annotation. For instance, the *Gene|Protein* type is more general than both *Gene* and *Protein*, whereas the *Chemical molecule* type is a hypernym of *Gene*, *Protein*, *Drug* and *Metabolite*. In the case of multiple annotations over the same span of text, we removed the more general labels, so that each NE has only one label. Contradictory cases, where two NERs label one NE with completely different tags, were not found.

After augmenting the existing NEs by running the two NER tools on the corpus, the outputs were combined to give a single "silver" annotation list. This operation was performed by computing the mathematical union of the three individual annotation sets, as shown in Equation 1.

$$\mathbb{A}_{\mathsf{Silver}} = \mathbb{A}_{\mathsf{UKPMC}} \cup \mathbb{A}_{\mathsf{Oscar}} \cup \mathbb{A}_{\mathsf{NeMine}} \quad (1)$$

Table 3 shows the ratios of named entities to the number of words in each subcorpus. The $\approx$ sign indicates strictly positive percentages, but which are rounded down to zero in this table for formatting purposes. In the four places where it occurs, the percentages lie between 0% and 0.005%,

[3] http://www.ncbi.nlm.nih.gov/nlmcatalog

[4] http://www.ncbi.nlm.nih.gov/pmc/tools/openftlist

| Type | UKPMC | NeMine | OSCAR |
|---|---|---|---|
| Gene | ✓ | ✓ | |
| Protein | ✓ | ✓ | |
| Gene\|Protein | ✓ | | |
| Disease | ✓ | ✓ | |
| Drug | ✓ | ✓ | |
| Metabolite | ✓ | ✓ | |
| Bacteria | | ✓ | |
| Diagnostic process | | ✓ | |
| General phenomenon | | ✓ | |
| Human phenomenon | | ✓ | |
| Indicator | | ✓ | |
| Natural phenomenon | | ✓ | |
| Organ | | ✓ | |
| Pathologic function | | ✓ | |
| Symptom | | ✓ | |
| Therapeutic process | | ✓ | |
| Chemical molecule | | | ✓ |
| Chemical adjective | | | ✓ |
| Enzyme | | | ✓ |
| Reaction | | | ✓ |

Table 2: Named entity types and their source.

exclusively. It can be observed that some entity types have approximately the same percentages in the two subdomains, e.g. phenomena and reactions. However, large differences can be observed in the case of some of the other entity types. For instance, chemical molecules occur twice as often in pharmacology articles than in cell biology, whereas proteins appear almost three times more often in cell biology than in pharmacology.

### 3.3 Experimental setup

Using the corpus described previously, we created a training set for supervised machine learning algorithms. Every document in the corpus was transformed into a vector consisting of 20 features. Each of these features corresponds to an entity type in Table 2, having a numeric value ranging from 0 to 1. This number represents the ratio of the specific entity type to the total number of named entities recognised in that document, as shown in Equation 2.

$$\theta = \frac{n_{type}}{N} \quad (2)$$

where $n_{type}$ represents the number of NEs of a certain type in a document and $N$ represents the total number of NEs in that document.

Furthermore, each vector was labelled with the subdomain to which the respective document belongs (i.e., cell biology or pharmacology).

Weka (Witten and Frank, 2005; Hall et al., 2009) was employed as the machine learning framework, due to its large variety of classification algorithms. We experimented with a large number of classifiers, ranging from Bayesian nets to functions, decision trees, decision rules and meta-classifiers. The best performing classifiers are shown in Table 4. BayesNet is an implementation of Bayesian Networks, SMO is an implementation of Support Vector Machines, J48 is an implementation of decision trees, whilst Jrip is an implementation of decision rules. Random Forest is an ensemble classifier that consists of many decision trees (in this study, J48 was used), outputting the class that occurs most frequently in the output of individual trees.

The baseline that has been used is ZeroR, a simple algorithm that classifies all instances as pertaining to the majority class. Since our classes have equal numbers of instances, the F-score of ZeroR is 50%.

| Type | CellBio | Pharma |
|---|---|---|
| Enzyme | 0.05% | 0.09% |
| Bacteria | 0.01% | 0.16% |
| Chemical adjective | ≈0% | ≈0% |
| Chemical molecule | 30.13% | 60.86% |
| Diagnose process | 0.03% | 0.23% |
| Disease | 3.35% | 4.27% |
| Drug | 1.25% | 2.83% |
| Gene | 0.87% | 1.09% |
| Gene\|Protein | 5.02% | 0.89% |
| General phenomenon | ≈0% | 0.01% |
| Human phenomenon | 0% | ≈0% |
| Indicator | 0.36% | 0.16% |
| Metabolite | 3.26% | 7.53% |
| Natural phenomenon | 0.02% | 0.1% |
| Organ | 0.09% | 0.27% |
| Pathologic function | 0.04% | 0.04% |
| Protein | 53.31% | 19.13% |
| Reaction | 1.71% | 1.31% |
| Symptom | 0.03% | 0.06% |
| Therapeutic process | 0.47% | 0.96% |

Table 3: Ratios of NE types to the total number of NEs in the two subdomains.

## 4 Results

The previously described features were used as input to various supervised machine learning algorithms; results and error analysis are provided in Section 4.1 and Section 4.2, respectively.

### 4.1 Experimental results

As can be seen from Table 4, Random Forest performs best, with 91.1% F-score. The other three classifiers give lower results, varying between 86% and 89.5%.

| Algorithm | P | R | $F_1$ |
|---|---|---|---|
| BayesNet | 89.5 | 89.4 | 89.4 |
| SMO | 86.1 | 86.1 | 86.1 |
| JRip | 87.8 | 87.8 | 87.8 |
| J48 | 86.8 | 86.8 | 86.8 |
| Random Forest | 91.3 | 91.1 | **91.1** |

Table 4: Classification results for the best-performing algorithms.

We also employed AdaBoost in conjunction with the previously mentioned four classifiers, and the results are given in Table 5. AdaBoost is a meta-algorithm that adapts itself during the course of several iterations in the sense that in each iteration, classifiers built are tweaked to correct those instances misclassified by prior classifiers. In this study, AdaBoost was run over 20 iterations, and it significantly improved the result of J48, by almost 4%, to 90.3%. However, AdaBoost decreased the F-score of Random Forest by 1% and that of BayesNet by 0.3%.

| Algorithm | P | R | $F_1$ |
|---|---|---|---|
| BayesNet | 89.2 | 89.2 | 89.2 |
| SMO | 86.1 | 86.1 | 86.1 |
| JRip | 87.9 | 87.9 | 87.9 |
| J48 | 90.3 | 90.3 | **90.3** |
| Random Forest | 90.3 | 90.1 | 90.1 |

Table 5: Classification results for AdaBoost in conjunction with the best-performing algorithms.

In order to determine which features have the most influence on classification, regardless of the classifying algorithm, two attribute evaluators were used to measure the information gain for each feature and to compute the value of the chi-squared statistic with respect to the class. The values obtained are shown in Table 6, and to illustrate their influence, are plotted in Figure 1, after being normalised.

Unsurprisingly, *Protein* is the feature with the most discriminatory power, considering it has the highest count and it occurs almost three times more often in the cell biology class than in the pharmacology class. *Chemical molecules* follow closely, again due to a high count and large difference between the classes. Due to their high scores obtained from the attribute evaluators, we ran the experiment again considering only these two features. The Random Forest classifier achieved an F-score of 80% using these parameters.

At the other end of the scale, there are five features which have very little influence in discriminating between the two classes. The corresponding named entity types have the lowest occurrence counts in the corpora, with the exception of *Organ*. When running Random Forest with these five features only, an F-score of 50.5% is obtained. This result is very close to the baseline, surpassing it by only a small fraction.

### 4.2 Error analysis

As can be seen in Table 7, a total of 64 papers were misclassified by the Random Forest classi-

| Attribute | InfoGain | ChiSquare |
|---|---|---|
| Protein | 0.4482 | 386.5648 |
| Chemical molecule | 0.3169 | 272.0111 |
| Gene\|Protein | 0.2265 | 211.8034 |
| Indicator | 0.1805 | 170.0186 |
| Gene | 0.1718 | 156.9504 |
| Metabolite | 0.1667 | 155.8135 |
| Reaction | 0.1545 | 144.6946 |
| Drug | 0.1301 | 124.2604 |
| Therapeutic process | 0.1259 | 111.4571 |
| Disease | 0.1189 | 111.1882 |
| Chemical adjective | 0.0642 | 55.5556 |
| Enzyme | 0.0473 | 41.089 |
| Diagnostic process | 0.0388 | 32.1161 |
| Bacteria | 0.0297 | 26.0522 |
| Natural phenomenon | 0.0227 | 20.8004 |
| Pathologic function | 0 | 0 |
| Symptom | 0 | 0 |
| General phenomenon | 0 | 0 |
| Organ | 0 | 0 |
| Human phenomenon | 0 | 0 |

Table 6: Attribute selection output from two attribute evaluators.

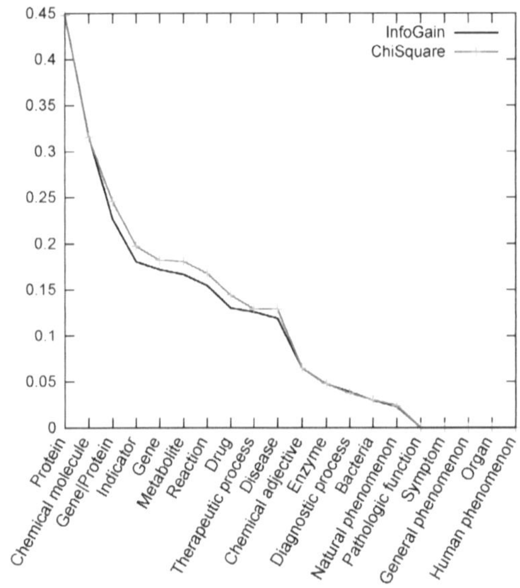


Figure 1: Normalised attribute selection output from two attribute evaluators.

fier, the best performing algorithm. Of these, 45 (i.e. 70%) are cell biology papers which were incorrectly classified as belonging to pharmacology, whilst the remaining 19 belong to the pharmacology class and are classified as cell biology.

| Labelled as | Cell_bio | Pharma |
|---|---|---|
| Cell_bio | 315 | 19 |
| Pharma | 45 | 341 |

Table 7: Confusion matrix for the Random Forest classifier.

As previously mentioned, the two features that achieved the highest information gain are the ratios for the *Protein* and *Chemical molecule* types. Accordingly, only these two features were considered in this error analysis.

We firstly examined the features of the cell biology documents which were incorrectly classified as pharmacology papers. It was noticeable that the majority of the misclassified documents in this case have a small percentage of *Proteins* (less than 0.35) and/or a large percentage of *Chemical molecules* (greater than 0.58). To confirm this observation, a sample of documents was accessed via the PubMed Central page which provides links to identified entities such as compounds, substances, genes and proteins. For instance, the misclassified cell biology paper with PMCID 2755470 was found to have no proteins, whilst the one with PMCID 2679709 has quite a large number of substances (chemical molecules).

We also analysed the features of papers in the pharmacology subdomain which were misclassified as cell biology documents. In contrast to the first type of misclassification, these documents have a large percentage of Proteins and/or small percentage of Chemical molecules. For example, the pharmacology paper with PMCID 2817930 contains many protein instances, whilst the one with PMCID 2680808 has no mentions of chemical molecules.

## 5 Conclusions and Future Work

We have shown that with the help of named entity identification, classifiers can be built that are able to distinguish between papers belonging to different biomedical subdomains. The Random Forest algorithm is able to discriminate between cell biology and pharmacology open-access full-text articles with an F-score of 91%. This result supports the hypothesis that sublanguages used in different biomedical domains exhibit significant semantic variations. Such variations should therefore be considered when adapting automated tools developed for a particular subdomain to new subdomains.

One possible future direction is to analyse multiple medical subdomains, such as neurology, virology and critical care. This could enable the measurement of the distance between various subdomains with respect to specific named entity types. Furthermore, a comparison of the method described above with those using bag-of-words or other non-semantic features could further enforce the importance of named entities in document classification and sublanguage identification.

## Acknowledgements

We would like to acknowledge the help given by Dr. C.J. Rupp in obtaining the collection of documents from the Open Access section of the UKMPC.

## References

Cecilia Arighi, Zhiyong Lu, Martin Krallinger, Kevin Cohen, W Wilbur, Alfonso Valencia, Lynette Hirschman, and Cathy Wu. 2011. Overview of the BioCreative III Workshop. *BMC Bioinformatics*, 12(Suppl 8):S1.

Kevin Bretonnel Cohen, Martha Palmer, and Lawrence Hunter. 2008. Nominalization and alternations in biomedical language. *PLoS ONE*, 3(9):e3158, 09.

Kevin Bretonnel Cohen, Dina Demner-Fushman, Sophia Ananiadou, John Pestian, Jun'ichi Tsujii, and Bonnie Webber, editors. 2009. *Proceedings of the BioNLP 2009 Workshop*. Association for Computational Linguistics, Boulder, Colorado, June.

Carol Friedman, Pauline Kra, and Andrey Rzhetsky. 2002. Two biomedical sublanguages: a description based on the theories of Zellig Harris. *Journal of Biomedical Informatics*, 35(4):222–235.

Mark Hall, Eibe Frank, Geoffrey Holmes, Bernhard Pfahringer, Peter Reutemann, and Ian H. Witten. 2009. The weka data mining software: An update. *SIGKDD Explorations*, 11(1).

Zellig Harris. 1968. *Mathematical Structures of Language*. John Wiley and Son, New York.

David Jessop, Sam Adams, Egon Willighagen, Lezan Hawizy, and Peter Murray-Rust. 2011. Oscar4: a flexible architecture for chemical text-mining. *Journal of Cheminformatics*, 3(1):41.

Jin-Dong Kim, Tomoko Ohta, and Jun'ichi Tsujii. 2008. Corpus annotation for mining biomedical events from literature. *BMC Bioinformatics*, 9(1):10.

Jin-Dong Kim, Yue Wang, Toshihisa Takagi, and Akinori Yonezawa. 2011. Overview of genia event task in bionlp shared task 2011. In *Proceedings of BioNLP Shared Task 2011 Workshop*, pages 7–15, Portland, Oregon, USA, June. Association for Computational Linguistics.

Martin Krallinger, Alexander Morgan, Larry Smith, Florian Leitner, Lorraine Tanabe, John Wilbur, Lynette Hirschman, and Alfonso Valencia. 2008. Evaluation of text-mining systems for biology: overview of the second biocreative community challenge. *Genome Biology*, 9(Suppl 2):S1.

Seth Kulick, Ann Bies, Mark Liberman, Mark Mandel, Ryan McDonald, Martha Palmer, Andrew Schein, and Lyle Ungar. 2004. Integrated annotation for biomedical information extraction. In *Proceedings of the BioLINK 2004*.

Thomas Lippincott, Diarmuid Seaghdha, and Anna Korhonen. 2011. Exploring subdomain variation in biomedical language. *BMC Bioinformatics*, 12(1):212.

Johanna R. McEntyre, Sophia Ananiadou, Stephen Andrews, William J. Black, Richard Boulderstone, Paula Buttery, David Chaplin, Sandeepreddy Chevuru, Norman Cobley, Lee-Ann Coleman, Paul Davey, Bharti Gupta, Lesley Haji-Gholam, Craig Hawkins, Alan Horne, Simon J. Hubbard, Jee-Hyub Kim, Ian Lewin, Vic Lyte, Ross MacIntyre, Sami Mansoor, Linda Mason, John McNaught, Elizabeth Newbold, Chikashi Nobata, Ernest Ong, Sharmila Pillai, Dietrich Rebholz-Schuhmann, Heather Rosie, Rob Rowbotham, C. J. Rupp, Peter Stoehr, and Philip Vaughan. 2010. UKPMC: a full text article resource for the life sciences. *Nucleic Acids Research*.

Ngan L. T. Nguyen and Jin-Dong Kim. 2008. Exploring domain differences for the design of pronoun resolution systems for biomedical text. In *Proceedings of the 22nd International Conference on Computational Linguistics - Volume 1*, COLING '08, pages 625–632, Stroudsburg, PA, USA. Association for Computational Linguistics.

Chikashi Nobata, Yutaka Sasaki, Noaki Okazaki, C. J. Rupp, Jun'ichi Tsujii, and Sophia Ananiadou. 2009. Semantic search on digital document repositories based on text mining results. In *International Conferences on Digital Libraries and the Semantic Web 2009 (ICSD2009)*, pages 34–48.

Martha Palmer, Daniel Gildea, and Paul Kingsbury. 2005. The proposition bank: An annotated corpus of semantic roles. *Computational Linguistics*, 31(1):71–105.

Sampo Pyysalo, Filip Ginter, Juho Heimonen, Jari Bjorne, Jorma Boberg, Jouni Jarvinen, and Tapio Salakoski. 2007. BioInfer: a corpus for information extraction in the biomedical domain. *BMC Bioinformatics*, 8(1):50.

Naomi Sager, Carol Friedman, and Margaret Lyman. 1987. *Medical Language Processing: Computer Management of Narrative Data*. Addison-Wesley, Reading, MA.

Yutaka Sasaki, Yoshimasa Tsuruoka, John McNaught, and Sophia Ananiadou. 2008. How to make the most of NE dictionaries in statistical NER. *BMC Bioinformatics*, 9(Suppl 11):S5.

Lorraine Tanabe, Natalie Xie, Lynne Thom, Wayne Matten, and W John Wilbur. 2005. GENETAG: a tagged corpus for gene/protein named entity recognition. *BMC Bioinformatics*, 6(Suppl 1):S3.

Paul Thompson, Syed Iqbal, John McNaught, and Sophia Ananiadou. 2009. Construction of an annotated corpus to support biomedical information extraction. *BMC Bioinformatics*, 10(1):349.

Paul Thompson, Raheel Nawaz, John McNaught, and Sophia Ananiadou. 2011. Enriching a biomedical event corpus with meta-knowledge annotation. *BMC Bioinformatics*, 12(1):393.

Karin Verspoor, Kevin Bretonnel Cohen, and Lawrence Hunter. 2009. The textual characteristics of traditional and open access scientific journals are similar. *BMC Bioinformatics*, 10(1):183.

Tuangthong Wattarujeekrit, Parantu Shah, and Nigel Collier. 2004. PASBio: predicate-argument structures for event extraction in molecular biology. *BMC Bioinformatics*, 5(1):155.

Ian Witten and Eibe Frank. 2005. *Data Mining: Practical Machine Learning Tools and Techniques (Second Edition)*. Morgan Kaufmann.

# Yet Another Language Identifier

**Martin Majliš**
Charles University in Prague
Institute of Formal and Applied Linguistics
Faculty of Mathematics and Physics
majlis@ufal.mff.cuni.cz

## Abstract

Language identification of written text has been studied for several decades. Despite this fact, most of the research is focused on a few most spoken languages, whereas the minor ones are ignored. The identification of a larger number of languages brings new difficulties that do not occur for a few languages. These difficulties are causing decreased accuracy. The objective of this paper is to investigate the sources of such degradation. In order to isolate the impact of individual factors, 5 different algorithms and 3 different number of languages are used. The Support Vector Machine algorithm achieved an accuracy of 98% for 90 languages and the YALI algorithm based on a scoring function had an accuracy of 95.4%. The YALI algorithm has slightly lower accuracy but classifies around 17 times faster and its training is more than 4000 times faster.

Three different data sets with various number of languages and sample sizes were prepared to overcome the lack of standardized data sets. These data sets are now publicly available.

## 1 Introduction

The task of language identification has been studied for several decades, but most of the literature is about identifying spoken language[1]. This is mainly because language identification of written form is considered an easier task, because it does not contain such variability as the spoken form, such as dialects or emotions.

Language identification is used in many NLP tasks and in some of them simple rules[2] are often good enough. But for many other applications, such as web crawling, question answering or multilingual documents processing, more sophisticated approaches need to be used.

This paper first discusses previous work in Section 2, and then presents possible hypothesis for decreased accuracy when a larger number of languages is identified in Section 3. Data used for experiments is described in Section 4, along with methods used in experiments for language identification in Section 5. Results for all methods as well as comparison with other systems is presented in Section 6.

## 2 Related Work

The methods used in language identification have changed significantly during the last decades. In the late sixties, Gold (1967) examined language identification as a task in automata theory. In the seventies, Leonard and Doddington (1974) was able to recognize five different languages, and in the eighties, Beesley (1988) suggested using cryptoanalytic techniques.

Later on, Cavnar and Trenkle (1994) introduced their algorithm with a sliding window over a set of characters. A list of the 300 most common n-grams for n in 1..5 is created during training for each training document. To classify a new document, they constructed a list of the 300 most common n-grams and compared n-grams position with the testing lists. The list with the least differences is the most similar one and new document is likely to be written in same language.

[1] `http://speech.inesc.pt/~dcaseiro/html/bibliografia.html`

[2] `http://en.wikipedia.org/wiki/Wikipedia:Language_recognition_chart`

They classified 3478 samples in 14 languages from a newsgroup and reported an achieved accuracy of 99.8%. This influenced many researches that were trying different heuristics for selecting n-grams, such as Martins and Silva (2005) which achieved an accuracy of 91.25% for 12 languages, or Hayati (2004) with 93.9% for 11 languages.

Sibun and Reynar (1996) introduced a method for language detection based on relative entropy, a popular measure also known as Kullback-Leibler distance. Relative entropy is a useful measure of the similarity between probability distributions. She used texts in 18 languages from the European Corpus Initiative CD-ROM. She achieved a 100% accuracy for bigrams.

In recent years, standard classification techniques such as support vector machines also became popular and many researchers used them Kruengkrai et al. (2005) or Baldwin and Lui (2010) for identifying languages.

Nowadays, language recognition is considered as an elementary NLP task[3] which can be used for educational purposes. McNamee (2005) used single documents for each language from project Gutenberg in 10 European languages. He preprocessed the training documents – the texts were lower-cased, accent marks were retained. Then, he computed a so-called profile of each language. Each profile consisted of a percentage of the training data attributed to each observed word. For testing, he used 1000 sentences per language from the Euro-parliament collection. To classify a new document, the same preprocessing was done and inner product based on the words in the document and the 1000 most common words in each language was computed. Performance varied from 80.0% for Portuguese to 99.5% for German.

Some researches such as Hughes et al. (2006) or Grothe et al. (2008) focused in their papers on the comparison of different approaches to language identification and also proposed new goals in that field, such as as minority languages or languages written non-Roman script.

Most of the researches in the past identified mostly up to twenty languages but in recent years, language identification of minority languages became the focus of Baldwin and Lui (2010), Choong et al. (2011), and Majliš (2012). All of them observed that the task became much harder for larger numbers of languages and accuracy of the system dropped.

[3]http://alias-i.com/lingpipe/demos/tutorial/langid/read-me.html

## 3 Hypothesis

The accuracy degradation with a larger number of languages in the language identification system may have many reasons. This section discusses these reasons and suggests how to isolate them. In some hypotheses, charts involving data from the W2C Wiki Corpus are used, which are introduced in Section 4.

### 3.1 Training Data Size

In many NLP applications, size of the available training data influences overall performance of the system, as was shown by Halevy et al. (2009).

To investigate the influence of training data size, we decided to use two different sizes of training data – 1 MB and 4 MB. If the drop in accuracy is caused by the lack of training data, then all methods used on 4 MB should outperform the same methods used on 1 MB of data.

### 3.2 Language Diversity

The increasing number of languages recognised by the system decreases language diversity. This may be another reason for the observed drop in the accuracy. We used information about language classes from the Ethnologue website (Lewis, 2009). The number of different language classes is depicted in Figure 1. *Class 1* represents the most distinguishable classes, such as Indo-European vs. Japonic, while *Class 2* represents finer classification, such as Indo-European, Germanic vs. Indo-European, Italic.

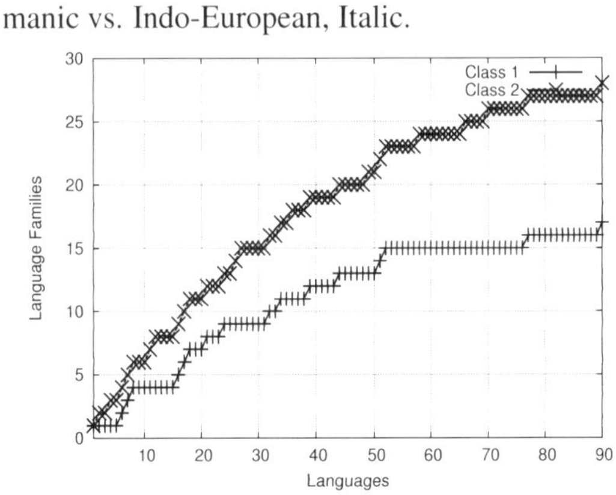


Figure 1: Language diversity on Wikipedia. Languages are sorted according to their text corpus size.

The first 52 languages belong to 15 different *Class 1* classes and the number of classes does not change until the 77th language, when the Swahili language from class Niger-Congo appears.

### 3.3 Scalability

Another issue with increasing number of languages is the scalability of used methods. There are several pitfalls for machine learning algorithms – a) many languages may require many features which may lead to failures caused by curse-of-dimensionality, b) differences in languages may shrink, so the classifier will be forced to learn minor differences and will lose its ability to generalise, and become overfitted, and c) the classifier may internally use only binary classifiers which may lead up to quadratic complexity (Dimitriadou et al., 2011).

## 4 Data Sets

For our experiments, we decided to use the W2C Wiki Corpus (Majliš, 2012) which contains articles from Wikipedia. The total size of all texts was 8 GB and available material for various languages differed significantly, as is displayed in Figure 2.

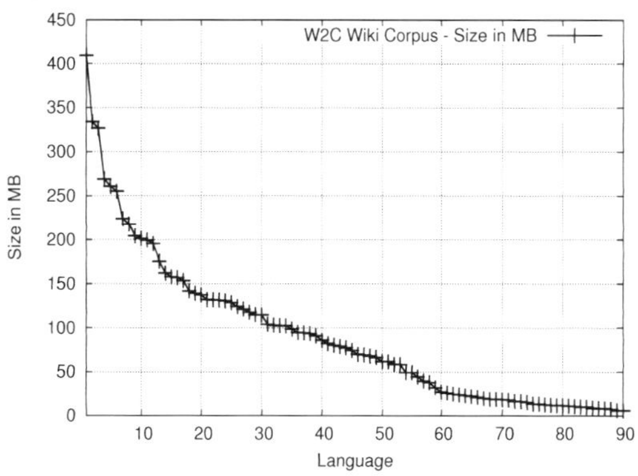


Figure 2: Available data in the W2C Wiki Corpus. Languages are sorted according to their size in the corpus.

We used this corpus to prepare 3 different data sets. We used one of them for testing hypothesis presented in the previous section and the remaining two for comparison with other systems. These data sets contain samples of length approximately 30, 140, and 1000 bytes. The sample of length 30 represents image caption or book title, the sample of length 140 represents tweet or user comment, and sample of length 1000 represents newspaper article.

All datasets are available at `http://ufal.mff.cuni.cz/~majlis/yali/`.

### 4.1 Long

The main purpose of this data set (*yali-dataset-long*) was testing hypothesis described in the previous section.

To investigate the drop, we intended to cover around 100 languages, but the amount of available data limited us. For example, the 80th language has 12 MB, whereas the 90th has 6 MB and tbe 100th has only 1 MB of text. To investigate the hypothesis of the influence of training data size, we decided to build a 1 MB and 4 MB corpus for each language, where the 1 MB corpus is a subset of the 4 MB one.

Then, we divided the corpus for each language into chunks with 1000 bytes of text, so we gained 1000 and 4000 chunks respectively. These chunks were divided into training and testing sets in a 90:10 ratio, thus we had 900 and 3600 training chunks, respectively, and 100 and 400 testing chunks respectively.

To reduce the risk that the training and testing are influenced by the position from which they were taken (the beginning or the end of the corpus), we decided to use every 10th sentence as a testing one and use the remaining ones for training.

Then, we created an n-gram for n in 1..4 frequency list for each language, each corpus size. From each frequency list, we preserved only the first m = 100 most frequent n-grams. For example, from the raw frequency list – a: 5, b: 3, c: 1, d: 1, and m = 2, frequency list a: 5, b: 3 would be created. We used this n-grams as features for testing classifiers.

### 4.2 Small

The second data set (*yali-dataset-small*) was prepared for comparison with Google Translate[4] (GT). The GT is paid service capable of recognizing 50 different languages. This data set contains 50 samples of lengths 30 and 140 for 48 languages, so it contains 4,800 samples in total.

### 4.3 Standard

The purpose of the third data sets is comparison with other systems for language identification. This data set contains 700 samples of length 30, 140, and 1000 for 90 languages, so it contains in total 189,000 samples.

[4] `http://translate.google.com`

| Size | L\N | 1 | 2 | 3 | 4 |
|---|---|---|---|---|---|
| 1MB | 30 | 177 | 1361 | 2075 | 2422 |
| | 60 | 182 | 1741 | 3183 | 4145 |
| | 90 | 186 | 1964 | 3943 | 5682 |
| 4MB | 30 | 176 | 1359 | 2079 | 2418 |
| | 60 | 182 | 1755 | 3184 | 4125 |
| | 90 | 187 | 1998 | 3977 | 5719 |

Table 1: The number of unique $N$-grams in corpus *Size* with $L$ languages. ($D^{(Size,L,n)}$)

## 5 Methods

To investigate the influence of the language diversity, we decided to use 3 different language counts – 30, 60, and 90 languages sorted according to their raw text size. For each corpus size ($cS \in \{1000, 4000\}$), language count ($lC \in \{30, 60, 90\}$), and n-gram size ($n \in \{1, 2, 3, 4\}$) we constructed a separate dictionary $D^{(cS,lC,n)}$ containing the first 100 most frequent n-grams for each language. The number of items in each dictionary is displayed in Table 1 and visualised for 1 MB corpus in Figure 3.

The dictionary sizes for 4 MB corpora were slightly higher when compared to 1 MB corpora, but surprisingly for 30 languages it was mostly opposite.

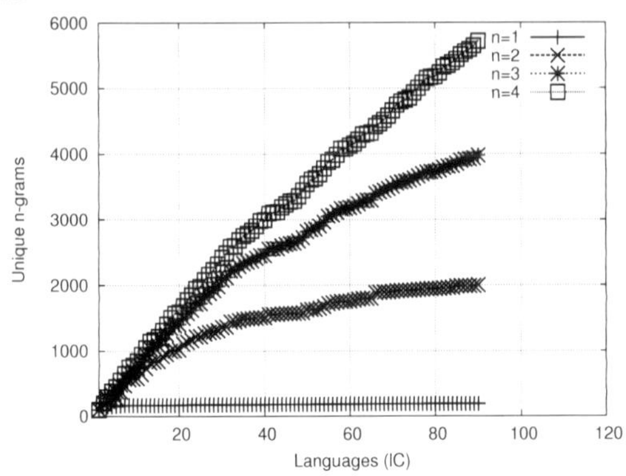


Figure 3: The number of unique n-grams in the dictionary $D^{(1000,lC,n)}$. Languages are sorted according to their text corpus size.

Then, we converted all texts into matrices in the following way. For each corpus size ($cS \in \{1000, 4000\}$), language count ($lC \in \{30, 60, 90\}$), and n-gram size ($n \in \{1, 2, 3, 4\}$) we constructed a training matrix $Tr^{(cS,lC,n)}$ and a testing matrix $Te^{(cS,lC,n)}$, where element on $Tr_{i,j}^{(cS,lC,n)}$ represents the number of occurrences of $j$-th n-gram from dictionary $D^{(cS,lC,n)}$ in training sample $i$, and $Tr_{i,0}^{(cS,lC,n)}$ represents language of that sample. The training matrix $Tr^{(cS,lC,n)}$ has dimension $(0.9 \cdot cS \cdot lC) \times (1 + \mid D^{(cS,lC,n)} \mid)$ and the testing matrix $Te^{(cS,lC,n)}$ has dimension $(0.1 \cdot cS \cdot lC) \times (1 + \mid D^{(cS,lC,n)} \mid)$.

For investigating the scalability of the different approaches to language identification, we decided to use five different methods. Three of them were based on standard classification algorithms and two of them were based on scoring function. For experimenting with the classification algorithms, we used R (2009) environment which contains many packages with machine learning algorithms[5], and for scoring functions we used Perl.

### 5.1 Support Vector Machine

The Suport Vector Machine (SVM) is a state of the art algorithm for classification. Hornik et al. (2006) compared four different implementations and concluded that Dimitriadou et al. (2011) implementation available in the package e1071 is the fastest one. We used SVM with sigmoid kernel, cost of constraints violation set to 10, and termination criterion set to 0.01.

### 5.2 Naive Bayes

The Naive Bayes classifier (NB) is a simple probabilistic classifier. We used Dimitriadou et al. (2011) implementation from the package e1071 with default arguments.

### 5.3 Regression Tree

Regression trees are implemented by Therneau et al. (2010) in the package rpart. We used it with default arguments.

### 5.4 W2C

The W2C algorithm is the same as was used by Majliš (2011). From the frequency list, probability is computed for each n-gram, which is used as a score in classification. The language with the highest score is the winning one. For example, from the raw frequency list – a: 5, b: 3, c: 1, d: 1, and m=2, the frequency list a: 5; b: 3, and computed scores – a: 0.5, b: 0.3 would be created.

[5] `http://cran.r-project.org/web/views/MachineLearning.html`

### 5.5 Yet Another Language Identifier

The Yet Another Language Identifier (YALI) algorithm is based on the W2C algorithm with two small modifications. The first is modification in n-gram score computation. The n-gram score is not based on its probability in raw data, but rather on its probability in the preserved frequency list. So for the numbers used in the W2C example, we would receive scores – a: 0.625, b: 0.375. The second modification is using rather byte n-grams instead of character n-grams.

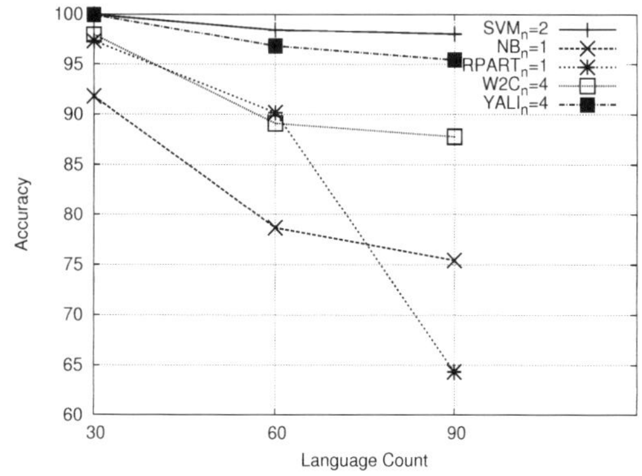


Figure 5: Accuracy for 1 MB corpus and the best *n*-gram length with respect to the number of languages.

## 6 Results & Discussion

At the beginning we used only data set *yali-dataset-long* to investigate the influence of various set-ups.

The accuracy of all experiments is presented in Table 2, and visualised in Figure 4 and Figure 5. These experiments also revealed that algorithms are strong in different situations. All classification techniques outperform all scoring functions on short n-grams and small amount of languages. However, with increasing n-gram length, their accuracy stagnated or even dropped. The increased number of languages is unmanageable for NB a RPART classifiers and their accuracy significantly decreased. On the other hand, the accuracy of scoring functions does not decrease so much with additional languages. The accuracy of the W2C algorithm decreased when greater training corpora was used or more languages were classified, whereas the YALI algorithm did not have these problems, but moreover its accuracy increased with greater training corpus.

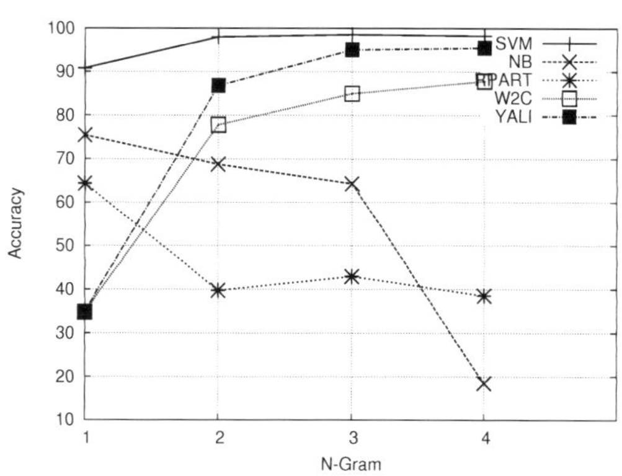


Figure 4: Accuracy for 90 languages and 1 MB corpus with respect to n-gram length.

The highest accuracy for all language amounts – 30, 60, 90 was achieved by the SVM with accuracies of 100%, 99%, and 98.5%, respectively, followed by the YALI algorithm with accuracies of 99.9%, 96.8%, and 95.4% respectively.

From the obtained results, it is possible to notice that 1 MB of text is sufficient for training language identifiers, but some algorithms achieved higher accuracy with more training material.

Our next focus was on the scalability of the used algorithms. Time required for training is presented in Table 3, and visualised in Figures 6 and 7.

The training of scoring functions required only loading dictionaries and therefore is extremely fast, whereas training classifiers required complicated computations. The scoring functions did not have any advantages, because all algorithms had to load all training examples, segment them, extract the most common n-grams, build dictionaries, and convert text to matrices as was described in Section 5.

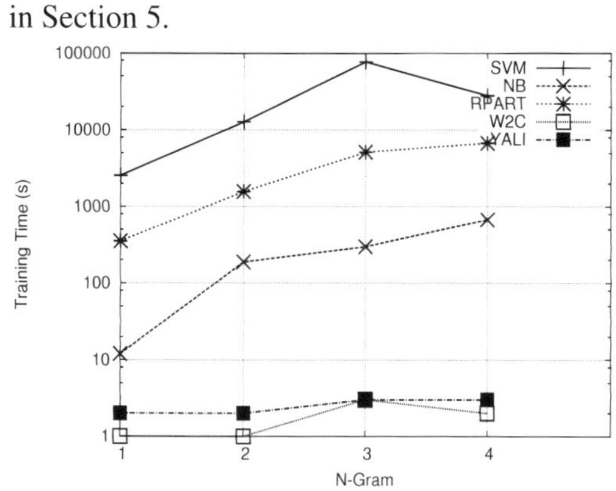


Figure 6: Training time for 90 languages and 1 MB corpus with respect to n-gram length.

| N-Gram | L | 1 | | 2 | | 3 | | 4 | |
|---|---|---|---|---|---|---|---|---|---|
| Method | S | 1MB | 4MB | 1MB | 4MB | 1MB | 4MB | 1MB | 4MB |
| SVM | 30 | 96.3% | 96.7% | 100.0% | 99.9% | 100.0% | 99.9% | 99.9% | 99.9% |
| | 60 | 91.5% | 92.3% | 98.5% | 98.5% | 99.0% | 99.0% | 98.6% | 98.5% |
| | 90 | 90.8% | 91.6% | 98.0% | 98.0% | 98.5% | - | 98.3% | - |
| NB | 30 | 91.8% | 94.2% | 91.3% | 90.9% | 82.2% | 93.3% | 32.1% | 59.9% |
| | 60 | 78.7% | 84.8% | 70.6% | 68.2% | 71.7% | 77.6% | 25.7% | 34.0% |
| | 90 | 75.4% | 82.7% | 68.8% | 66.5% | 64.3% | 71.0% | 18.4% | 17.5% |
| RPART | 30 | 97.3% | 96.7% | 98.8% | 98.6% | 98.4% | 97.8% | 97.7% | 97.4% |
| | 60 | 90.2% | 91.2% | 67.3% | 72.0% | 67.2% | 68.8% | 65.5% | 74.6% |
| | 90 | 64.3% | 55.9% | 39.7% | 39.6% | 43.0% | 44.0% | 38.5% | 39.6% |
| W2C | 30 | 38.0% | 38.6% | 89.9% | 91.0% | 96.2% | 96.5% | 97.9% | 98.1% |
| | 60 | 34.7% | 30.9% | 83.0% | 81.7% | 86.0% | 84.9% | 89.1% | 82.0% |
| | 90 | 34.7% | 30.9% | 77.8% | 77.6% | 84.9% | 83.4% | 87.8% | 82.7% |
| YALI | 30 | 38.0% | 38.6% | 96.7% | 96.2% | 99.6% | 99.5% | 99.9% | 99.8% |
| | 60 | 35.0% | 31.2% | 86.1% | 86.1% | 95.7% | 96.4% | 96.8% | 97.4% |
| | 90 | 34.9% | 31.1% | 86.8% | 87.8% | 95.0% | 95.6% | 95.4% | 96.1% |

Table 2: Accuracy of classifiers for various corpora sizes, n-gram lengths, and language counts.

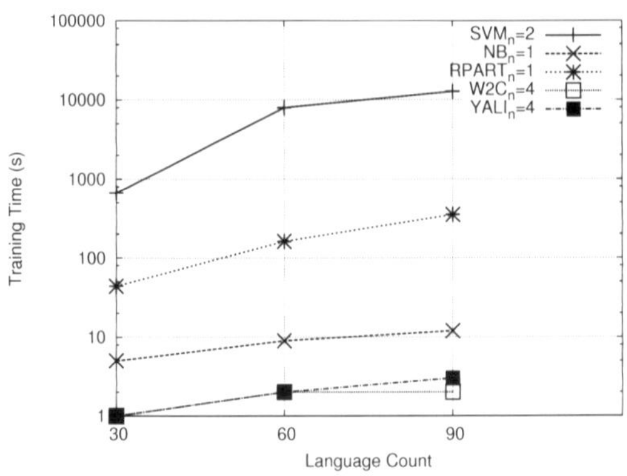


Figure 7: Training time for 1 MB corpus and the best $n$-gram length with respect to the number of languages.

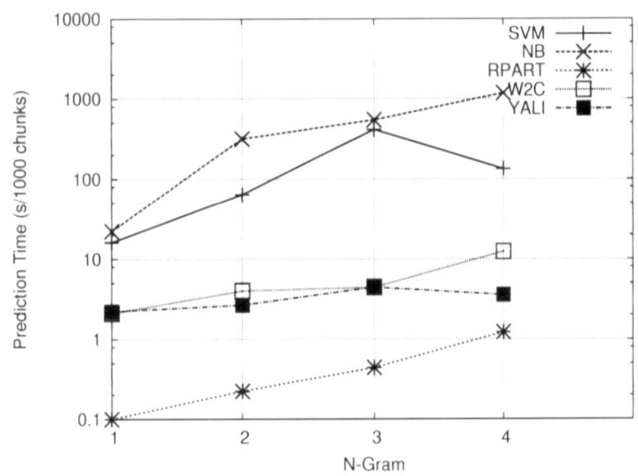


Figure 8: Prediction time for 90 languages and 1 MB corpus with respect to n-gram length.

Time required for training increased dramatically for SVM and RPART algorithms when the number of languages or the corpora size increased. It is possible to use the SVM only with unigrams or bigrams, because training on trigrams required 12 times more time for 60 languages compared with 30 languages. The SVM also had problems with increasing corpora sizes, because it took almost 10-times more time when the corpus size increased 4 times. Scoring functions scaled well and were by far the fastest ones. We terminated training the SVM on trigrams and quadgrams for 90 languages after 5 days of computation.

Finally, we also measured time required for classifying all testing examples. The results are in Table 4, and visualised in Figure 8 and Figure 6. Times displayed in the table and charts represents the number of seconds needed for classifying 1000 chunks.

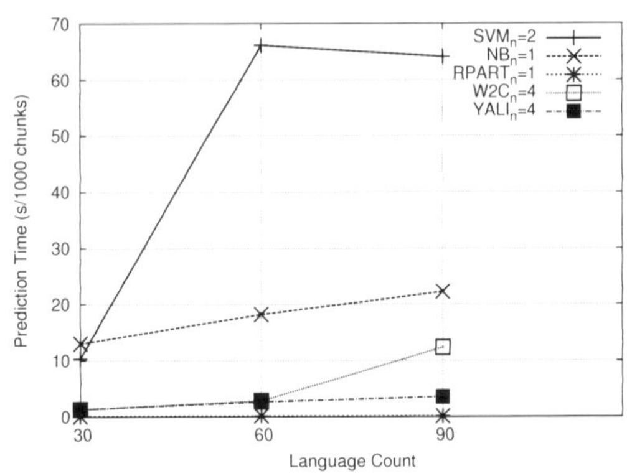


Prediction time for 1 MB corpus and the best $n$-gram length with respect to the number of languages.

The RPART algorithm was the fastest classifier followed by both scoring functions, whereas NB was the slowest one. All algorithms with 4 times more data achieved slightly higher accuracy, but their training took 4 times longer, with the exception of the SVM which took at least 10 times longer. The SVM algorithm is the least scalable

| N-Gram | L | 1 | | 2 | | 3 | | 4 | |
|---|---|---|---|---|---|---|---|---|---|
| Method | S | 1MB | 4MB | 1MB | 4MB | 1MB | 4MB | 1MB | 4MB |
| SVM | 30 | 215 | 1858 | 663 | 1774 | 627 | 7976 | 655 | 3587 |
| | 60 | 1499 | 13653 | 7981 | 87260 | 7512 | 44288 | 26943 | 207123 |
| | 90 | 2544 | 24841 | 12698 | 267824 | 76693 | - | 27964 | - |
| NB | 30 | 5 | 19 | 27 | 83 | 40 | 144 | 54 | 394 |
| | 60 | 9 | 32 | 76 | 255 | 142 | 515 | 363 | 1187 |
| | 90 | 12 | 56 | 188 | 683 | 298 | 1061 | 672 | 2245 |
| RPART | 30 | 44 | 189 | 144 | 946 | 267 | 1275 | 369 | 1360 |
| | 60 | 162 | 1332 | 736 | 3447 | 1270 | 11114 | 2583 | 7493 |
| | 90 | 351 | 1810 | 1578 | 7647 | 5139 | 23413 | 6736 | 17659 |
| W2C | 30 | 1 | 1 | 0 | 1 | 0 | 1 | 1 | 1 |
| | 60 | 1 | 2 | 1 | 2 | 2 | 1 | 2 | 2 |
| | 90 | 1 | 1 | 1 | 1 | 3 | 1 | 2 | 1 |
| YALI | 30 | 1 | 1 | 1 | 1 | 1 | 1 | 1 | 1 |
| | 60 | 2 | 2 | 2 | 2 | 2 | 2 | 2 | 0 |
| | 90 | 2 | 1 | 2 | 1 | 3 | 1 | 3 | 2 |

Table 3: Training Time

| Method | | 30 | 60 | 90 |
|---|---|---|---|---|
| | Acc | 100.0% | 98.5% | 98.0% |
| SVM | Tre | 663 | 7981 | 12698 |
| n=2 | Pre | 10.3 | 66.2 | 64.1 |
| | Acc | 91.8% | 78.7% | 75.4% |
| NB | Tre | 5 | 9 | 12 |
| n=1 | Pre | 13.0 | 18.2 | 22.2 |
| | Acc | 97.3% | 90.2% | 64.3% |
| RPART | Tre | 44 | 162 | 351 |
| n=1 | Pre | 0.1 | 0.2 | 0.1 |
| | Acc | 97.9% | 89.1% | 87.8% |
| W2C | Tre | 1 | 2 | 2 |
| n=4 | Pre | 1.3 | 2.8 | 12.3 |
| | Acc | 99.9% | 96.8% | 95.4% |
| YALI | Tre | 1 | 2 | 3 |
| n=4 | Pre | 1.3 | 2.7 | 3.6 |

Table 5: Comparison of classifiers with best parameters. Label *Acc* represents accuracy, *Tre* represents training time in seconds, and *Pre* represents prediction time for 1000 chunks in seconds.

algorithm of all the examined – all the rest required proportionally more time for training and prediction when the greater training corpus was used or more languages were classified.

The comparison of all methods is presented in Table 5. For each model we selected the n-grams size with the best trade-off between accuracy and time required for training and prediction. The two most accurate algorithms are SVM and YALI. The SVM achieved the highest accuracy for all languages but its training took around 4000 times longer and classification was around 17 times slower than the YALI.

In the next step we evaluated the YALI algorithm for various size of selected n-grams. These

| | Languages | | |
|---|---|---|---|
| Size | 30 | 140 | 1000 |
| 100 | 64.9% | 85.7 % | 93.8 % |
| 200 | 68.7% | 87.3 % | 93.9 % |
| 400 | 71.7% | 88.0 % | 94.0 % |
| 800 | 73.7% | 88.5 % | 94.0 % |
| 1600 | 75.0% | 88.8% | 94.0% |

Table 6: Effect of the number of selected 4-grams on accuracy.

experiments were evaluated on the data set *yali-dataset-standard*. Achieved results are presented in Table 6. The number of used n-grams increased the accuracy for short samples from 64.9% to 75.0% but it had no effect on long samples.

As the last step in evaluation we decided to compare the YALI with Google Translate (GT), which also provides language identification for 50 languages through their API.[6] For comparison we used data set *yali-dataset-small* which contains 50 samples of length 30 and 140 for each language (4800 samples in total). Achieved results are presented in Table 7. The GT and the YALI perform comparably well on samples of length 30 on which they achieved accuracy 93.6% and 93.1% respectively, but on samples of length 140 GT with accuracy 97.3% outperformed YALI with accuracy 94.8%.

## 7 Conclusions & Future Work

In this paper we compared 5 different algorithms for language identification – three based on the

[6] `http://code.google.com/apis/language/translate/v2/using_rest.html`

| N-Gram | L | 1 | | 2 | | 3 | | 4 | |
|---|---|---|---|---|---|---|---|---|---|
| Method | S | 1MB | 4MB | 1MB | 4MB | 1MB | 4MB | 1MB | 4MB |
| SVM | 30 | 3.7 | 7.3 | 10.3 | 6.8 | 9.0 | 31.8 | 9.3 | 13.8 |
| | 60 | 13.3 | 30.1 | 66.2 | 189.7 | 59.8 | 92.8 | 236.7 | 375.2 |
| | 90 | 16.1 | 36.7 | 64.1 | 381.4 | 414.9 | - | 133.4 | - |
| NB | 30 | 13.0 | 13.6 | 75.3 | 77.1 | 132.7 | 147.9 | 186.0 | 349.7 |
| | 60 | 18.2 | 18.8 | 155.3 | 162.0 | 291.5 | 297.4 | 860.3 | 676.0 |
| | 90 | 22.2 | 24.7 | 318.1 | 251.9 | 546.3 | 469.3 | 1172.8 | 1177.8 |
| RPART | 30 | 0.1 | 0.1 | 0.3 | 0.1 | 0.1 | 0.2 | 0.7 | 0.2 |
| | 60 | 0.2 | 0.1 | 0.2 | 0.0 | 0.2 | 0.4 | 0.8 | 0.2 |
| | 90 | 0.1 | 0.1 | 0.2 | 0.1 | 0.4 | 0.3 | 1.2 | 0.3 |
| W2C | 30 | 0.7 | 0.8 | 1.7 | 1.6 | 3.3 | 1.5 | 1.3 | 2.2 |
| | 60 | 1.3 | 1.3 | 2.2 | 2.4 | 2.7 | 2.5 | 2.8 | 2.9 |
| | 90 | 2.1 | 1.8 | 4.0 | 3.2 | 4.4 | 3.8 | 12.3 | 5.8 |
| YALI | 30 | 0.7 | 0.8 | 1.0 | 1.2 | 2.0 | 1.9 | 1.3 | 2.2 |
| | 60 | 1.3 | 1.5 | 1.8 | 2.2 | 2.5 | 2.2 | 2.7 | 2.5 |
| | 90 | 2.2 | 1.8 | 2.7 | 2.9 | 4.4 | 3.5 | 3.6 | 3.7 |

Table 4: Prediction Time

| | | Text Length | |
|---|---|---|---|
| | | 30 | 140 |
| System | Google | 93.6% | 97.3% |
| | YALI | 93.1% | 94.8% |

Table 7: Comparison of Google Translate and YALI on 48 languages.

standard classification algorithms (Support Vector Machine (SVM), Naive Bayes (NB), and Regression Tree (RPART)) and two based on scoring functions. For investigating the influence of the amount of training data we constructed two corpora from the Wikipedia with 90 languages. To investigate the influence of number if identified languages we created three sets with 30, 60, and 90 languages. We also measured time required for training and classification.

Our experiments revealed that the standard classification algorithms requires at most bigrams while the scoring ones required quadgrams. We also showed that Regression Trees and Naive Bayes are not suitable for language identification because they achieved accuracy 64.3% and 75.4% respectively.

The best classifier for language identification was the SVM algorithm which achieved accuracy 98% for 90 languages but its training took 4200 times more and its classification was 16 times slower than the YALI algorithm with accuracy 95.4%. This YALI algorithm has also potential for increasing accuracy and number of recognized languages because it scales well.

We also showed that the YALI algorithm is comparable with the Google Translate system. Both systems achieved accuracy 93% for samples of length 30. On samples of length 140 Google Translate with accuracy 97.3% outperformed YALI with accuracy 94.8%.

All data sets as well as source codes are available at `http://ufal.mff.cuni.cz/~majlis/yali/`.

In the future we would like to focus on using described techniques not only on recognizing languages but also on recognizing character encodings which is directly applicable for web crawling.

## Acknowledgments

The research has been supported by the grant Khresmoi (FP7-ICT-2010-6-257528 of the EU and 7E11042 of the Czech Republic).

## References

[Baldwin and Lui2010] Timothy Baldwin and Marco Lui. 2010. *Language identification: the long and the short of the matter.* Human Language Technologies: The 2010 Annual Conference of the North American Chapter of the Association for Computational Linguistics, pp. 229–237.

[Beesley1988] Kenneth R. Beesley. 1988. *Language identifier: A computer program for automatic natural-language identification of on-line text.* Languages at Crossroads: Proceedings of the 29th Annual Conferenceof the American Translators Association, 12-16 October 1988, pp. 47-54.

[Cavnar and Trenkle1994] William B. Cavnar and John M. Trenkle. 1994. *N-gram-based text categoriza-*

*tion*. In Proceedings of Symposium on Document Analysis and Information Retrieval.

[Choong et al.2011] Chew Yew Choong, Yoshiki Mikami, and Robin Lee Nagano. 2011. *Language Identification of Web Pages Based on Improved N gram Algorithm*. IJCSI, issue 8, volume 3.

[Dimitriadou et al.2011] Evgenia Dimitriadou, Kurt Hornik, Friedrich Leisch, David Meyer, and and Andreas Weingessel 2011. *e1071: Misc Functions of the Department of Statistics (e1071), TU Wien*. R package version 1.5-27. `http://CRAN.R-project.org/package=e1071`.

[Gold1967] E. Mark Gold. 1967. *Language identification in the limit*. Information and Control, 5:447474.

[Grothe et al.2008] Lena Grothe, Ernesto William De Luca, and Andreas Nrnberger. 2008. *A Comparative Study on Language Identification Methods*. Proceedings of the Sixth International Language Resources and Evaluation (LREC'08). Marrakech, 980-985.

[Halevy et al.2009] Alon Halevy, Peter Norvig, and Fernando Pereira. 2009. *The unreasonable effectiveness of data*. IEEE Intelligent Systems, 24:8–12.

[Hayati 2004] Katia Hayati. 2004. Language Identification on the World Wide Web. Master Thesis, University of California, Santa Cruz. `http://lily-field.net/work/masters.pdf`.

[Hornik et al.2006] Kurt Hornik, Alexandros Karatzoglou, and David Meyer. 2006. *Support Vector Machines in R*. Journal of Statistical Software 2006., 15.

[Hughes et al.2006] Baden Hughes, Timothy Baldwin, Steven Bird, Jeremy Nicholson, and Andrew Mackinlay. 2006. *Reconsidering language identification for written language resources*. Proceedings of LREC2006, 485–488.

[Kruengkrai et al.2005] Canasai Kruengkrai, Prapass Srichaivattana, Virach Sornlertlamvanich, and Hitoshi Isahara. 2005. *Language identification based on string kernels*. In Proceedings of the 5th International Symposium on Communications and Information Technologies (ISCIT2005), pages 896899, Beijing, China.

[Leonard and Doddington1974] Gary R. Leonard and George R. Doddington. 1974. *Automatic language identification*. Technical report RADC-TR-74-200, Air Force Rome Air Development Center.

[Lewis2009] M. Paul Lewis. 2009. *Ethnologue: Languages of the World, Sixteenth edition*. Dallas, Tex.: SIL International. Online version: `http://www.ethnologue.com/`

[McNamee2005] Paul McNamee. 2005. *Language identification: a solved problem suitable for undergraduate instruction*. J. Comput. Small Coll, volume: 20, issue: 3, February 2005, 94–101. Consortium for Computing Sciences in Colleges, USA.

[Majliš2012] Martin Majliš, Zdeněk Žabokrtský. 2012. *Language Richness of the Web*. In Proceedings of the Eight International Language Resources and Evaluation (LREC'12), Istanbul, Turkey, May 2012.

[Majliš2011] Martin Majliš. 2011. *Large Multilingual Corpus*. Mater Thesis, Charles University in Prague.

[Martins and Silva2005] Bruno Martins and Mário J. Silva. 2005. Language identification in web pages. Proceedings of the 2005 ACM symposium on Applied computing, SAC '05, 764–768. ACM, New York, NY, USA. `http://doi.acm.org/10.1145/1066677.1066852`.

[R2009] R Development Core Team. 2009. *R: A Language and Environment for Statistical Computing*. R Foundation for Statistical Computing. ISBN 3-900051-07-0. `http://www.R-project.org`,

[Sibun and Reynar1996] Penelope Sibun and Jeffrey C. Reynar. 1996. *Language identification: Examining the issues*. In Proceedings of the 5th Symposium on Document Analysis and Information Retrieval.

[Therneau et al.2010] Terry M. Therneau, Beth Atkinson, and R port by Brian Ripley. 2010. *rpart: Recursive Partitioning*. R package version 3.1-48. `http://CRAN.R-project.org/package=rpart`.

# Discourse Type Clustering using POS *n*-gram Profiles and High-Dimensional Embeddings

**Christelle Cocco**
Department of Computer Science and Mathematical Methods
University of Lausanne
Switzerland
Christelle.Cocco@unil.ch

## Abstract

To cluster textual sequence types (discourse types/modes) in French texts, K-means algorithm with high-dimensional embeddings and fuzzy clustering algorithm were applied on clauses whose POS (part-of-speech) *n*-gram profiles were previously extracted. Uni-, bi- and trigrams were used on four 19th century French short stories by Maupassant. For high-dimensional embeddings, power transformations on the chi-squared distances between clauses were explored. Preliminary results show that high-dimensional embeddings improve the quality of clustering, contrasting the use of bi- and trigrams whose performance is disappointing, possibly because of feature space sparsity.

## 1 Introduction

The aim of this research is to cluster textual sequence types (named here discourse types)[1], such as narrative, descriptive, argumentative and so on in French texts, and especially in short stories which could contain all types.

For this purpose, texts were segmented into clauses (section 2.1). To cluster the latter, *n*-gram POS (part-of-speech) tag profiles were extracted (section 2.3). POS-tags were chosen because of their expected relation to discourse types.

Several authors have used POS-tags among other features for various text classification tasks, such as Biber (1988) for text type detection, Karlgren and Cutting (1994) and Malrieu and Rastier (2001) for genre classification, and Palmer et al. (2007) for situation entity classification. The latter is an essential component of English discourse modes (Smith, 2009). Moreover, previous work in discourse type detection has shown a dependency between POS-tags and these types (Cocco et al., 2011).

In this paper, K-means algorithm with high-dimensional embeddings and fuzzy clustering algorithm were applied on uni-, bi- and trigram POS-tag profiles (section 2.4) and results were evaluated (section 2.5). Finally, results are given in section 3.

## 2 Method

### 2.1 Expert assessment

The human expert, a graduate student in French linguistics, annotated 19th century French short stories by Maupassant, using XML tags. Each text was first segmented into clauses, whose length is typically shorter than sentences. Then, texts were annotated retaining the following six discourse types: narrative, argumentative, descriptive, explicative, dialogal and injunctive.[2] They resulted from an adaptation of the work of Adam (2008a; 2008b) in text and discourse analysis, as well as Bronckart (1996) in psycholinguistics, concerning textual sequence types. The former does not consider the injunctive type.

Let us briefly describe these types (Adam, 2008a; Adam, 2008b; Bronckart, 1996), together with the criteria finally adopted by the human expert for this time-consuming task.

[1]**Sequence** type is an appropriate name, because it refers to text **passage** type. However, it will be further mentioned as discourse types, a frequent French term. In English, a standard term is: discourse modes.

[2]Regarding English, there are five discourse modes according to Smith (2009): narrative, description, report, information and argument.

**Narrative** type corresponds to told narrative. One of the principal linguistic markers of this type is the presence of past historic tense. However, when referring to repeated actions, imperfect tense is generally used. **Argumentative** type corresponds to texts whose aim is to convince somebody of an argument. An important linguistic marker of this type is the presence of argumentative connectors such as *mais* "but", *cependant* "however", *pourtant* "yet" and so on. **Explicative** type aims to explain something unknown, such as encyclopaedic knowledge, and answers to the question "Why?". A typical linguistic marker of this type is the presence of phraseological phrases, such as *(si)...c'est parce que/c'est pour que* "(if)...it is because/in order to". **Descriptive** type represents textual parts where the time of the story stops and where characteristic properties of a subject, animated or not, are attributed. Several linguistic markers are relevant for this type: use of imperfect tense (except when the narrative part is in present tense); a large number of adjectives; spatio-temporal organizers; and stative verbs. **Dialogal** type is a verbal exchange. However, in this project, direct speech is considered as dialogal too. Typical linguistic markers of this type are quotes, strong punctuation and change of spatio-temporal frame. Finally, **injunctive** type is an incentive for action. This type has linguistic markers such as use of imperative tense and exclamation marks. In our corpus, this type is always included in a dialogal segment.

Discourse types are generally nested inside each other resulting in a hierarchical structure. For instance, an injunctive sequence of one clause length can be included in a dialogal sequence, which can in turn be included in a longer narrative sequence matching the entire text. In the simplified treatment attempted here, the problem is linearized: only the leaves of the hierarchical structure will be considered.

## 2.2 Corpus

The corpus consists of four $19^{\text{th}}$ century French short stories by Maupassant: "L'Orient" , "Le Voleur", "Un Fou?" and "Un Fou". Descriptive statistics about these texts are given in table 1. These values are based on unigram counts. For bigram and trigram counts, clauses shorter than two and three words respectively were removed. For the first text, "L'Orient", three clauses were removed for trigrams; for "Le Voleur", one clause was removed for trigrams; and for "Un Fou?", thirteen clauses for trigrams. An extra step was made for "Un Fou", because of its very different structure w.r.t. the three other texts. Indeed, the majority of this text is written as a diary. Dates, which could not be attributed to a discourse type, were consequently removed, reducing the number of clauses from 401 to 376 for unigrams. Then, two clauses were removed for bigrams because they were too short, and again ten for trigrams.

## 2.3 Preprocessing

Before applying clustering algorithms, annotated texts were preprocessed to obtain a suitable contingency table, and dissimilarities between clauses were computed. Firstly, each text was POS-tagged with TreeTagger (Schmid, 1994) excluding XML tags. Secondly, using the manual clause segmentation made by the human expert, distributions over POS-tag $n$-grams were obtained for each clause, resulting in a contingency table.

Then, chi-squared distances between clauses were computed. In order to accomplish this, coordinates of the contingency table (with $n_{ik}$ denoting the number of objects common to clause $i$ and POS-tag $n$-gram $k$, $n_{i\bullet} = \sum_k n_{ik}$ and $n_{\bullet k} = \sum_i n_{ik}$) are transformed in this manner:

$$y_{ik} = \frac{e_{ik}}{f_i\sqrt{\rho_k}} - \sqrt{\rho_k} \qquad (1)$$

where $e_{ik} = n_{ik}/n$ are the relative counts, $f_i = e_{i\bullet} = n_{i\bullet}/n$ (row weights) and $\rho_k = e_{\bullet k} = n_{\bullet}k/n$ (column weights) are the margin counts. Finally, the squared Euclidean distances between these new coordinates

$$D_{ij} = \sum_k (y_{ik} - y_{jk})^2 \qquad (2)$$

define the chi-squared distances.

## 2.4 Algorithms

Two algorithms were applied on these distances.

**K-means with high-dimensional embedding**

Firstly, the well-known K-means (see *e.g.* Manning and Schütze (1999)) was performed in a weighted version (*i.e.* longer clauses are more important than shorter ones), by iterating the following pair of equations:

$$z_i^g = \begin{cases} 1 & \text{if} \quad g = \underset{h}{\text{argmin}}\, D_i^h \\ 0 & \text{else.} \end{cases} \qquad (3)$$

| Texts | ♯ sent. | ♯ clauses | ♯ tokens | | ♯ types | | % discourse types according to the expert | | | | | |
|---|---|---|---|---|---|---|---|---|---|---|---|---|
| | | | with punct. | w/o punct. | word | tag | arg | descr | dial | expl | inj | nar |
| L'Orient | 88 | 189 | 1'749 | 1'488 | 654 | 27 | 4.23 | 20.11 | 25.93 | 19.05 | 2.65 | 28.04 |
| Le Voleur | 102 | 208 | 1'918 | 1'582 | 667 | 29 | 4.81 | 12.02 | 13.94 | 4.81 | 2.88 | 61.54 |
| Un Fou? | 150 | 314 | 2'625 | 2'185 | 764 | 28 | 18.15 | 10.51 | 14.65 | 14.65 | 8.28 | 33.76 |
| Un Fou | 242 | 376 | 3'065 | 2'548 | 828 | 29 | 17.82 | 13.83 | 1.86 | 11.70 | 12.23 | 42.55 |

Table 1: Statistics of the annotated texts by Maupassant. For the text "Un Fou", dates were initially removed from the text. Number of sentences as considered by TreeTagger (Schmid, 1994). Number of clauses as segmented by the human expert. Number of tokens including punctuation and compounds as tagged by TreeTagger. Number of tokens without punctuation and numbers, considering compounds as separated tokens. Number of wordform types. Number of POS-tag types. The last columns give the percentage of clauses for each discourse type (arg = argumentative, descr = descriptive, dial = dialogal, expl = explicative, inj = injunctive, nar = narrative).

$$D_i^g = \sum_j f_j^g D_{ij} - \Delta_g \qquad (4)$$

where $z_i^g$ is the membership of clause $i$ in group $g$ and $D_i^g$ is the chi-squared distance between the clause $i$ and the group $g$ as resulting from the *Huygens principle*. In the equation 4, $f_j^g = (f_i z_{ig})/\rho_g = p(i|g)$, $D_{ij}$ is the chi-squared distances between clauses given by the equation 2 and $\Delta_g = 1/2 \sum_{jk} f_j^g f_k^g D_{jk}$ is the inertia of group $g$. In addition, $\rho_g = \sum_i f_i z_{ig} = p(g)$ is the relative weight of group $g$.

At the outset, the membership matrix $Z$ was chosen randomly, and then the iterations were computed until stabilisation of the matrix $Z$ or a number of maximum iterations $N_{\max}$.

Besides the K-means algorithm, Schoenberg transformations $\varphi(D)$ were also operated. They transform the original squared Euclidean distances $D$ into new squared Euclidean distances $\varphi(D)$ (Bavaud, 2011) and perform a high-dimensional embedding of data, similar to those used in Machine Learning. Among all Schoenberg transformations, the simple componentwise power transformation was used, *i.e.*

$$\varphi(D_{ij}) = (D_{ij})^q \qquad (5)$$

where $0 < q \leq 1$.

In a nutshell, the K-means algorithm was applied on the four texts, for uni-, bi- and trigrams POS-tags, with $q$ in equation 5 varying from 0.1 to 1 with steps of 0.05. Given that the aim was to find the six groups annotated by the human expert, the K-means algorithm was computed with a number of groups $m = 6$. Moreover, $N_{\max} = 400$ and for each $q$, calculations were run 300 times, and then the averages of the relevant quantities (see section 2.5) were computed.

**Fuzzy clustering**

Secondly, the same algorithm which was used in a previous work (Cocco et al., 2011) was applied here, *i.e.* the fuzzy clustering algorithm.

In brief, it consists of iterating, as for the K-means, the membership $z_i^g$ of clause $i$ in group $g$ defined in the following way (Rose et al., 1990; Bavaud, 2009):

$$z_i^g = \frac{\rho_g \exp(-\beta D_i^g)}{\sum_{h=1}^{m} \rho_h \exp(-\beta D_i^h)} \qquad (6)$$

until stabilisation of the membership matrix $Z$ (randomly chosen at the beginning as uniformly distributed over the $m$ groups) or after $N_{\max}$ iterations. $D_i^g$ is given by equation 4 and $\rho_g$ is the relative weight of group $g$. Moreover, it turns out convenient to set $\beta := 1/(t_{\text{rel}} \times \Delta)$, the "inverse temperature" parameter, where $\Delta := \frac{1}{2} \sum_{ij} f_i f_j D_{ij}$ is the inertia and $t_{\text{rel}}$ is the relative temperature which must be fixed in advance.

The values of $\beta$ controls for the bandwidth of the clustering, *i.e.* the number of groups: the higher $\beta$, the larger the final number of groups $M$ (see figure 9). As a matter of fact, depending of $\beta$ values, group profiles are more or less similar. Also, group whose profiles are similar enough are aggregated, reducing the number of groups from $m$ (initial number of groups chosen at the beginning) to $M$. This aggregation is made by adding memberships of clauses: $z_i^{[g \cup h]} = z_i^g + z_i^h$. Two groups are considered similar enough if $\theta_{gh}/\sqrt{\theta_{gg}\theta_{hh}} \geq 1 - 10^{-5}$, with $\theta_{gh} = \sum_{i=1}^{n} f_i z_i^g z_i^h$ which measures the overlap between $g$ and $h$ (Bavaud, 2010). Finally, each clause is attributed to the most probable group.

For the application in this project, fuzzy clustering algorithm was computed on the four texts, for uni- bi- and trigrams POS-tags. At the outset, the initial number of groups $m$ was equal to the number of clauses for each text (see table 1 and section 2.2), with a relative temperature $t_{\text{rel}}$ from 0.022 to 0.3 with steps of 0.001 (except for the text "Un Fou" with $t_{\text{rel min}} = 0.02$, $t_{\text{rel max}} = 0.3$ and $t_{\text{rel step}} = 0.01$). Besides this, $N_{\text{max}} = 400$ and for each $t_{\text{rel}}$, algorithm was run 20 times, and finally the averages of the relevant quantities (see section 2.5) were computed.

### 2.5 Evaluation criteria

The clustering obtained by the two algorithms (K-means with high-dimensional embedding and fuzzy clustering) were compared to the classification made by the human expert. As clustering induces anonymous partitions, traditional indices such as precision, recall and Cohen's Kappa cannot be computed.

Among the numerous similarity indices between partitions, we have examined the *Jaccard index* (Denœud and Guénoche, 2006; Youness and Saporta, 2004):

$$J = \frac{r}{r+u+v} \qquad (7)$$

whose values vary between 0 and 1, and the *corrected Rand index* (Hubert and Arabie, 1985; Denœud and Guénoche, 2006):

$$RC = \frac{r - \text{Exp}(r)}{\text{Max}(r) - \text{Exp}(r)} \qquad (8)$$

whose the maximal value is 1. When this index equals 0, it means that similarities between partitions stem from chance. However, it can also take negative values when number of similarities is lower than the expectation (*i.e.* chance).

Both indices are based upon the contingency table $n_{ij}$, defined by the number of objects attributed simultaneously to group $i$ (w.r.t. the first partition) and to group $j$ (w.r.t. the second partition). Moreover, in both indices, $r = \frac{1}{2}\sum_{ij} n_{ij}(n_{ij} - 1)$ is the number of pairs simultaneously joined together, $u = \frac{1}{2}(\sum_j n_{\bullet j}^2 - \sum_{ij} n_{ij}^2)$ (respectively $v = \frac{1}{2}(\sum_i n_{i\bullet}^2 - \sum_{ij} n_{ij}^2)$) is the number of pairs joined (respectively separated) in the partition obtained with algorithm and separated (respectively joined) in the partition made by the human expert, $\text{Exp}(r) = \frac{1}{2n(n-1)}\sum_i n_{i\bullet}(n_{i\bullet} - 1)\sum_j n_{\bullet j}(n_{\bullet j} - 1)$ is the expected number of pairs simultaneously joined together by chance and $\text{Max}(r) = \frac{1}{4}\sum_i n_{i\bullet}(n_{i\bullet} - 1) + \sum_j n_{\bullet j}(n_{\bullet j} - 1)$.

## 3 Results

On the one hand, results obtained with the K-means algorithm and power ($q$) transformations for uni-, bi- and trigrams are presented in figures 1 to 8. On the other hand, results obtained with fuzzy clustering for uni- bi- and trigrams are only shown for the text "Le Voleur" in figures 9 to 13. For the three other texts, results will be discussed below.

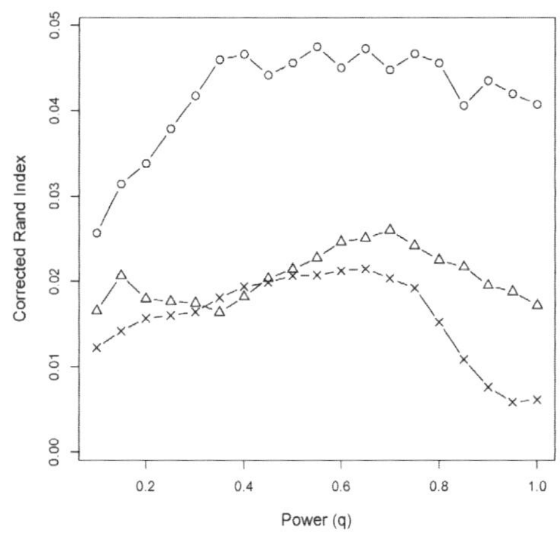


Figure 1: "L'Orient" with K-means algorithm: corrected rand index as a function of power (q) (○ = unigrams, △ = bigrams and × = trigrams). The standard deviation is approximatively constant across $q$ ranging from a minimum of 0.018 and a maximum of 0.024 (unigrams); 0.0099 and 0.015 (bigrams); 0.0077 and 0.013 (trigrams).

A first remark is that corrected Rand index and Jaccard index behave differently in general. This difference is a consequence of the fact that Jaccard index does not take into account the number of pairs simultaneously separated in the two partitions, a fact criticised by Milligan and Cooper (1986).

Regarding the texts "L'Orient", "Le Voleur" and "Un Fou?" with K-means algorithm and the corrected Rand index (figures 1, 3 and 5), unigrams give the best results. Moreover, power transformations (equation 5) tend to improve them. For instance, for the text "L'Orient" (figure 1), the best result is $RC = 0.048$ with $q = 0.55$, and for the text "Un Fou?" (figure 5), the best

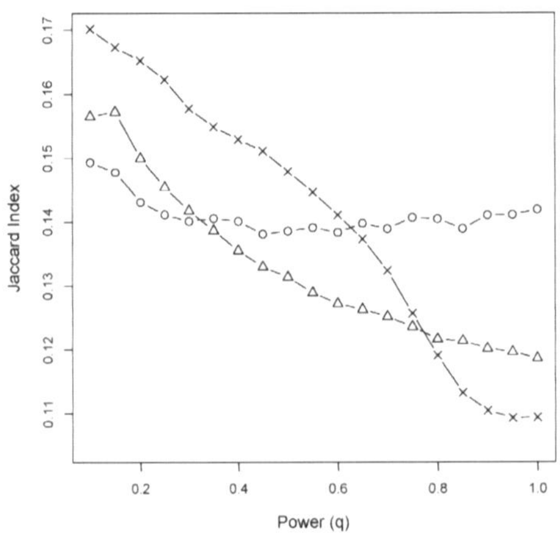


Figure 2: "L'Orient" with K-means algorithm: Jaccard index as a function of power (q) (○ = unigrams, △ = bigrams and × = trigrams).

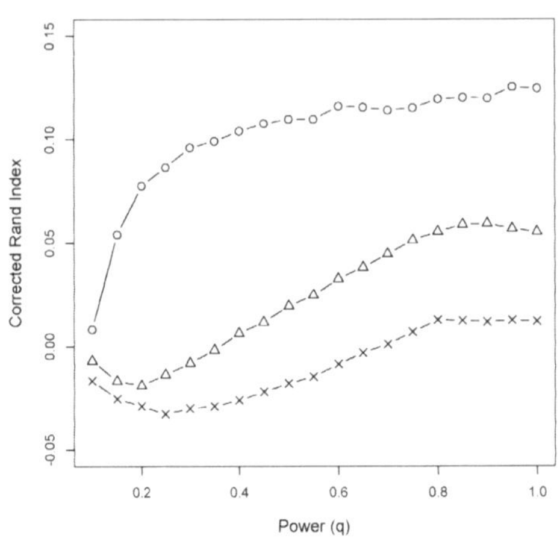


Figure 3: "Le Voleur" with K-means algorithm: corrected rand index as a function of power (q) (○ = unigrams, △ = bigrams and × = trigrams).

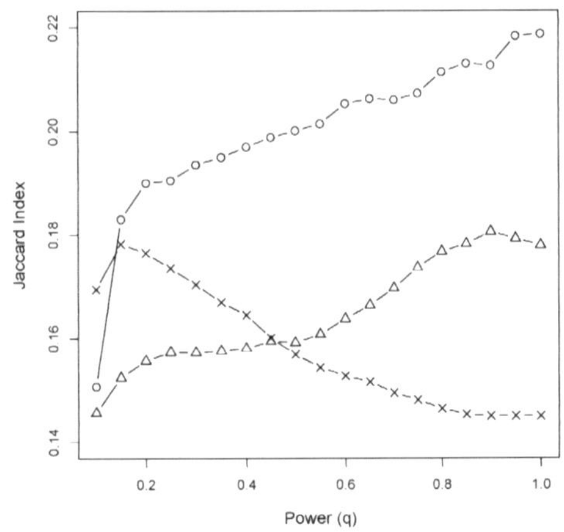


Figure 4: "Le Voleur" with K-means algorithm: Jaccard index as a function of power (q) (○ = unigrams, △ = bigrams and × = trigrams).

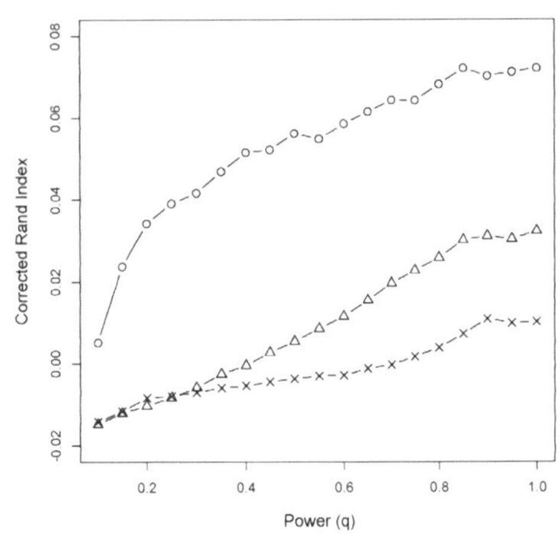


Figure 5: "Un Fou?" with K-means algorithm: corrected rand index as a function of power (q) (○ = unigrams, △ = bigrams and × = trigrams).

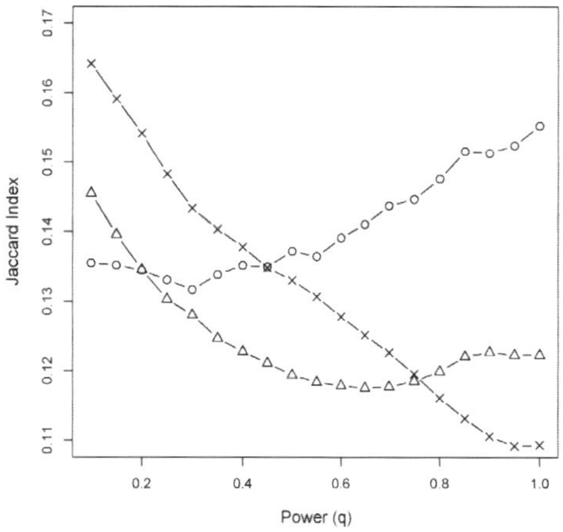


Figure 6: "Un Fou?" with K-means algorithm: Jaccard index as a function of power (q) (○ = unigrams, △ = bigrams and × = trigrams).

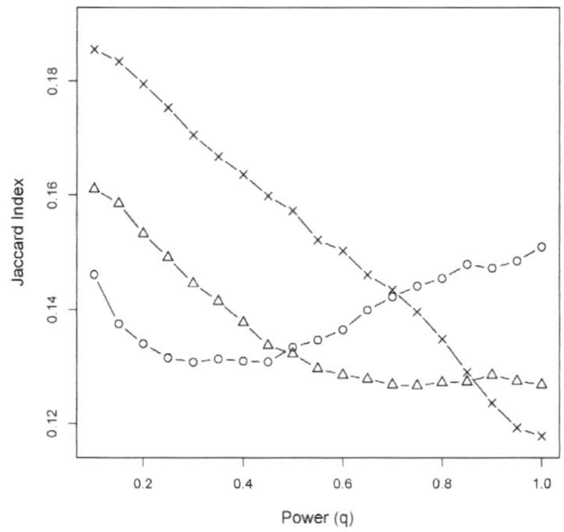


Figure 8: "Un Fou" with K-means algorithm: Jaccard index as a function of power (q) (○ = unigrams, △ = bigrams and × = trigrams).

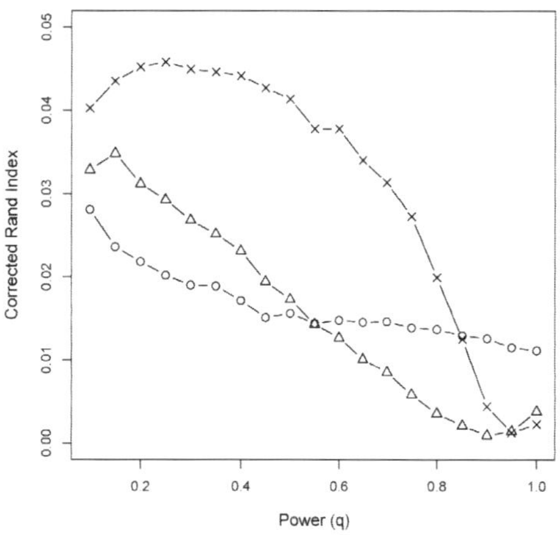


Figure 7: "Un Fou" with K-means algorithm: corrected rand index as a function of power (q) (○ = unigrams, △ = bigrams and × = trigrams).

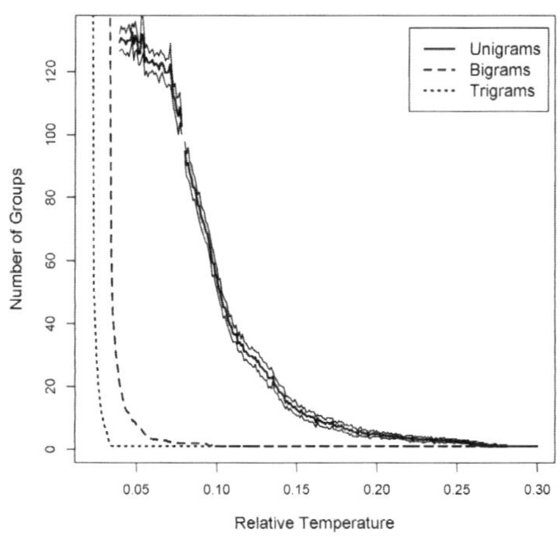


Figure 9: "Le Voleur" with fuzzy clustering algorithm: average number of groups as a function of the relative temperature. For unigrams, the thick line indicates the average and the two thin lines represent the standard deviation. The other curves depict the average of the number of groups.

result is $RC = 0.072$ with $q = 0.85$.

Regarding the fuzzy clustering algorithm, figure 9 shows, for the text "Le Voleur", the relation between the relative temperature and the number of groups for uni- bi- and trigrams, *i.e.* number of groups decreases when relative temperature increases. Figure 10 (respectively figure 12) presents the corrected Rand index (respectively the Jaccard index) as a function of relative temperature, while figure 11 (respectively figure 13) shows, for each relative temperature, the average number of groups on the x-axis and the average corrected Rand index (respectively Jaccard index) on the y-axis, over 20 clusterings. There is a remarkable peak for this text ($RC = 0.31$ (respectively $J = 0.48$)), when $t_{\text{rel}} = 0.145$ (respectively $0.148$), corresponding to $M = 14.4$ (respectively $13.4$). The same phenomenon appears with the text "Un Fou?", when $t_{\text{rel}} = 0.158$ and $M = 7.8$. However, the peak for the Jaccard index is less important and it is not the highest value. More-

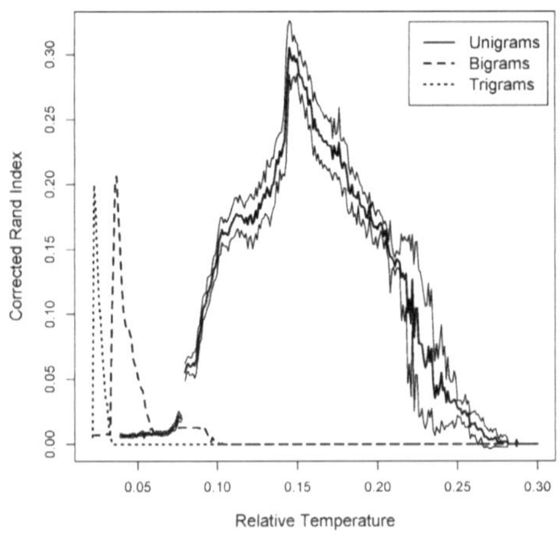


Figure 10: "Le Voleur" with fuzzy clustering algorithm: corrected Rand index as a function of relative temperature.

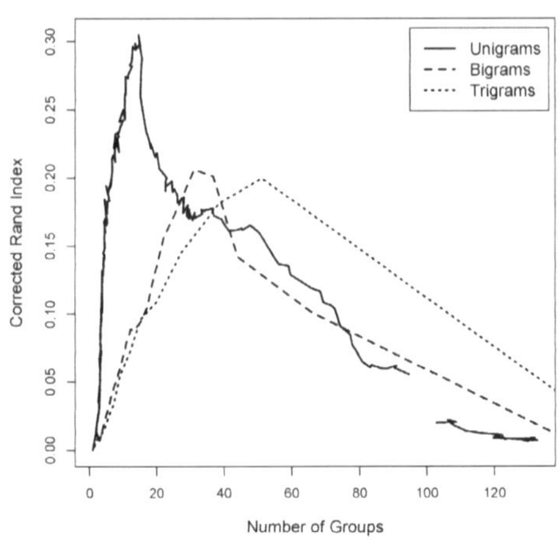


Figure 11: "Le Voleur" with fuzzy clustering algorithm: corrected Rand index as a function of number of groups.

over, for the latter text, there is a higher peak, which occurs only with the corrected Rand index, for $t_{\text{rel}} = 0.126$ and $M = 24.5$.

For the two other texts, there are some peaks, but not as marked as in other texts. Besides, for these two texts, corrected Rand index takes negative values, especially for "Un Fou". While the reason for these different behaviours is not known, it should be noted that the structure of these texts is different from that of the two other texts. Indeed, "Un Fou" is written as a diary and uses mainly the present tense, also in narrative and

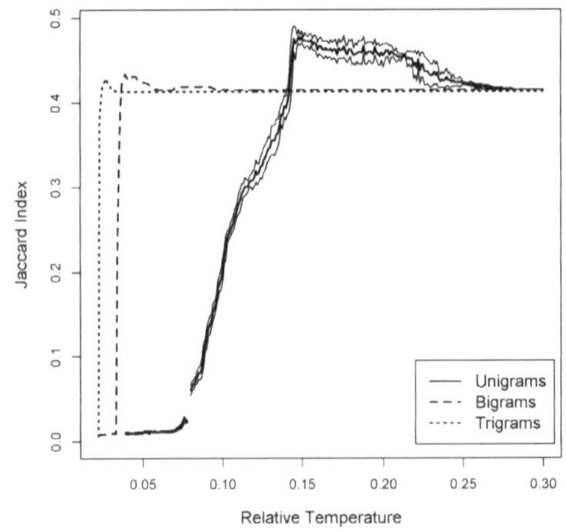


Figure 12: "Le Voleur" with fuzzy clustering algorithm: Jacccard index as a function of relative temperature.

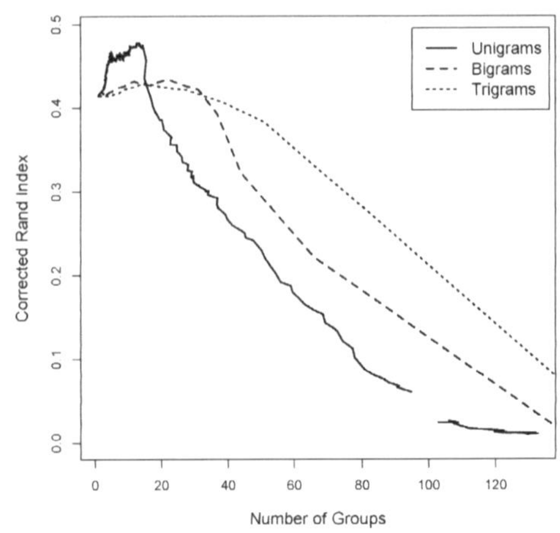


Figure 13: "Le Voleur" with fuzzy clustering algorithm: Jaccard index as a function of number of groups.

descriptive parts; "L'Orient" contains several long monologues mainly using the present tense too.

On figure 12, it appears that Jaccard index is constant when one group remains, and the same phenomenon appears for all texts. Indeed, from the distribution of table 2, one finds from equation 7: $r = 8\,939$, $u = 0$ and $v = 12\,589$, implying $J = 0.415$.

Overall, it is clear that results differ depending on texts, no matter which algorithm or evaluation criterion is used. Furthermore, they are always better for "Le Voleur" than for the three

| arg | descr | dial | expl | inj | nar |
|---|---|---|---|---|---|
| 10 | 25 | 29 | 10 | 6 | 128 |

Table 2: Types distribution for the text "Le Voleur".

other texts.

Finally, in most case, unigrams give better results than bi- and tri-grams. The relatively disappointing performance of bi- and trigrams (w.r.t. unigrams) could be accounted for by the sparsity of the feature space and the well-known associated "curse of dimensionality", in particular in clustering (see *e.g.* Houle et al. (2010)). Results are clearly different for "Un Fou", and the reason of this difference still needs to be investigated.

Certainly, as the sample is small and there is a unique annotator, all these results must be considered with caution.

## 4 Conclusion and further development

A first conclusion is that the use of POS-tag *n*-grams does not seem to improve the solution of the problem exposed here. In contrast, high-dimensional embedding seems to improve results. Concerning evaluation criteria, results clearly vary according to the selected index, which makes it difficult to compare methods. Another point is that even choosing only short stories of one author, text structures can be very different and certainly do not give the same results.

These results are interesting and in general better than those found in a previous work (Cocco et al., 2011), but this is still work in progress, with much room for improvement. A next step would be to combine fuzzy clustering with high-dimensional embedding, which can both improve results. Moreover, it could be interesting to add typical linguistic markers, such as those mentioned in section 2.1, or stylistic features. It would also be possible to use lemmas instead of or with POS-tags, if more data could be added to the corpus. Besides, *Cordial Analyseur* [3] could be used instead of TreeTagger, because it provides more fine-grained POS-tags. However, as for *n*-grams, it could imply a sparsity of the feature space. Another idea would be to perform a supervised classification with cross-validation. In this case, it would be interesting to investigate feature selection (see *e.g.* Yang and Pedersen (1997)). Also, the hierarchical structure of texts (cf. section 2.1) should be explored. Only the leaves were considered here, but in reality, one clause belongs to several types depending on the hierarchical level examined. Therefore, it could be relevant to consider the dominant discourse type instead of the leaf discourse type. Similarly, since in our corpus, injunctive type is always included in dialogal type, the former could be removed to obtain a larger dialogal class. In addition, it would be useful to find a better adapted measure of similarity between partitions. Finally, an important improvement would be to obtain more annotated texts, which should improve results, and a second human expert, which would permit us to assess the difficulty of the task.

[3] `http://www.synapse-fr.com/Cordial_Analyseur/Presentation_Cordial_Analyseur.htm`

## Acknowledgments

I would like to thank François Bavaud and Aris Xanthos for helpful comments and useful discussions; Guillaume Guex for his help with technical matters; and Raphaël Pittier for annotating the gold standard.

## References

Jean-Michel Adam. 2008a. *La linguistique textuelle: Introduction à l'analyse textuelle des discours*. Armand Colin, Paris, 2nd edition.

Jean-Michel Adam. 2008b. *Les textes: types et prototypes*. Armand Colin, Paris, 2nd edition.

François Bavaud. 2009. Aggregation invariance in general clustering approaches. *Advances in Data Analysis and Classification*, 3(3):205–225.

François Bavaud. 2010. Euclidean distances, soft and spectral clustering on weighted graphs. In José Balcázar, Francesco Bonchi, Aristides Gionis, and Michèle Sebag, editors, *Machine Learning and Knowledge Discovery in Databases*, volume 6321 of *Lecture Notes in Computer Science*, pages 103–118. Springer, Berlin; Heidelberg.

François Bavaud. 2011. On the Schoenberg transformations in data analysis: Theory and illustrations. *Journal of Classification*, 28(3):297–314.

Douglas Biber. 1988. *Variation across Speech and Writing*. Cambridge University Press.

Jean-Paul Bronckart. 1996. *Activité langagière, textes et discours: Pour un interactionisme socio-discursif*. Delachaux et Niestlé, Lausanne; Paris.

Christelle Cocco, Raphaël Pittier, François Bavaud, and Aris Xanthos. 2011. Segmentation and clustering of textual sequences: a typological approach.

In *Proceedings of the International Conference Recent Advances in Natural Language Processing 2011*, pages 427–433, Hissar, Bulgaria, September. RANLP 2011 Organising Committee.

Guy de Maupassant. 1882. Le voleur. *Gil Blas*, June 21. http://un2sg4.unige.ch/athena/selva/maupassant/textes/voleur.html. Thierry Selva. Accessed 2011, July 6.

Guy de Maupassant. 1883. L'orient. *Le Gaulois*, September 13. http://un2sg4.unige.ch/athena/selva/maupassant/textes/orient.html. Thierry Selva. Accessed 2011, March 5.

Guy de Maupassant. 1884. Un fou?. *Le Figaro*, September 1. http://un2sg4.unige.ch/athena/maupassant/maup_fou.html. Thierry Selva. Accessed 2011, February 7.

Guy de Maupassant. 1885. Un fou. *Le Gaulois*, September 2. http://un2sg4.unige.ch/athena/selva/maupassant/textes/unfou.html. Thierry Selva. Accessed 2011, April 26.

Lucile Denœud and Alain Guénoche. 2006. Comparison of distance indices between partitions. In Vladimir Batagelj, Hans-Hermann Bock, Anuška Ferligoj, and Aleš Žiberna, editors, *Data Science and Classification*, Studies in Classification, Data Analysis, and Knowledge Organization, pages 21–28. Springer Berlin Heidelberg.

Michael Houle, Hans-Peter Kriegel, Peer Kröger, Erich Schubert, and Arthur Zimek. 2010. Can shared-neighbor distances defeat the curse of dimensionality? In Michael Gertz and Bertram Ludäscher, editors, *Scientific and Statistical Database Management*, volume 6187 of *Lecture Notes in Computer Science*, pages 482–500. Springer, Berlin; Heidelberg.

Lawrence Hubert and Phipps Arabie. 1985. Comparing partitions. *Journal of Classification*, 2(1):193–218.

Jussi Karlgren and Douglass Cutting. 1994. Recognizing text genres with simple metrics using discriminant analysis. In *Proceedings of the 15th conference on Computational linguistics*, volume 2 of *COLING '94*, pages 1071–1075, Stroudsburg, PA, USA. Association for Computational Linguistics.

Denise Malrieu and Francois Rastier. 2001. Genres et variations morphosyntaxiques. *Traitement automatique des langues*, 42(2):547–577.

Christopher D. Manning and Hinrich Schütze. 1999. *Foundations of Statistical Natural Language Processing*. The MIT Press, 1st edition, June.

Glenn W. Milligan and Martha C. Cooper. 1986. A study of the comparability of external criteria for hierarchical cluster analysis. *Multivariate Behavioral Research*, 21(4):441–458.

Alexis Palmer, Elias Ponvert, Jason Baldridge, and Carlota Smith. 2007. A sequencing model for situation entity classification. In *Proceedings of the 45th Annual Meeting of the Association of Computational Linguistics*, pages 896–903, Prague, Czech Republic, June.

Kenneth Rose, Eitan Gurewitz, and Geoffrey C. Fox. 1990. Statistical mechanics and phase transitions in clustering. *Physical Review Letters*, 65(8):945–948.

Helmut Schmid. 1994. Probabilistic part-of-speech tagging using decision trees. In *Proceedings of the International Conference on New Methods in Language Processing*, pages 44–49.

Carlota S. Smith. 2009. *Modes of Discourse: The Local Structure of Texts*. Number 103 in Cambridge studies in linguistics. Cambridge University Press, Cambridge, UK, digitally printed version edition.

Yiming Yang and Jan O. Pedersen. 1997. A comparative study on feature selection in text categorization. In *Proceedings of the 14th International Conference on Machine Learning*, pages 412–420.

Genane Youness and Gilbert Saporta. 2004. Une Méthodologie pour la Comparaison de Partitions. *Revue de Statistique Appliquée*, 52(1):97–120.

# Hierarchical Bayesian Language Modelling for the Linguistically Informed

**Jan A. Botha**
Department of Computer Science
University of Oxford, UK
jan.botha@cs.ox.ac.uk

## Abstract

In this work I address the challenge of augmenting n-gram language models according to prior linguistic intuitions. I argue that the family of hierarchical Pitman-Yor language models is an attractive vehicle through which to address the problem, and demonstrate the approach by proposing a model for German compounds. In an empirical evaluation, the model outperforms the Kneser-Ney model in terms of perplexity, and achieves preliminary improvements in English-German translation.

## 1 Introduction

The importance of effective language models in machine translation (MT) and automatic speech recognition (ASR) is widely recognised. n-gram models, in particular ones using Kneser-Ney (KN) smoothing, have become the standard workhorse for these tasks. These models are not ideal for languages that have relatively free word order and/or complex morphology. The ability to encode additional linguistic intuitions into models that already have certain attractive properties is an important piece of the puzzle of improving machine translation quality for those languages. But despite their widespread use, KN n-gram models are not easily extensible with additional model components that target particular linguistic phenomena.

I argue in this paper that the family of hierarchical Pitman-Yor language models (HPYLM) (Teh, 2006; Goldwater et al., 2006) are suitable for investigations into more linguistically-informed n-gram language models. Firstly, the flexibility to specify arbitrary back-off distributions makes it easy to incorporate multiple models into a larger n-gram model. Secondly, the Pitman-Yor process prior (Pitman and Yor, 1997) generates distributions that are well-suited to a variety of power-law behaviours, as is often observed in language. Catering for a variety of those is important since the frequency distributions of, say, suffixes, could be quite different from that of words. KN smoothing is less flexibility in this regard. And thirdly, the basic inference algorithms have been parallelised (Huang and Renals, 2009), which should in principle allow the approach to still scale to large data sizes.

As a test bed, I consider compounding in German, a common phenomenon that creates challenges for machine translation into German.

## 2 Background and Related Work

n-gram language models assign probabilities to word sequences. Their key approximation is that a word is assumed to be fully determined by $n-1$ words preceding it, which keeps the number of independent probabilities to estimate in a range that is computationally attractive. This basic model structure, largely devoid of syntactic insight, is surprisingly effective at biasing MT and ASR systems toward more fluent output, given a suitable choice of target language.

But the real challenge in constructing n-gram models, as in many other probabilistic settings, is how to do smoothing, since the vast majority of linguistically plausible n-grams will occur rarely or be absent altogether from a training corpus, which often renders empirical model estimates misleading. The general picture is that probability mass must be shifted away from some events and redistributed across others.

The method of Kneser and Ney (1995) and

its later modified version (Chen and Goodman, 1998) generally perform best at this smoothing, and are based on the idea that the number of distinct contexts a word appears in is an important factor in determining the probability of that word. Part of this smoothing involves discounting the counts of n-grams in the training data; the modified version uses different levels of discounting depending on the frequency of the count. These methods were designed with surface word distributions, and are not necessarily suitable for smoothing distributions of other kinds of surface units.

Bilmes and Kirchhoff (2003) proposed a more general framework for n-gram language modelling. Their Factored Language Model (FLM) views a word as a vector of features, such that a particular feature value is generated conditional on some history of preceding feature values. This allowed the inclusion of n-gram models over sequences of elements like PoS tags and semantic classes. In tandem, they proposed more complicated back-off paths; for example, trigrams can back-off to two underlying bigram distributions, one dropping the left-most context word and the other the right-most. With the right combination of features and back-off structure they got good perplexity reductions, and obtained some improvements in translation quality by applying these ideas to the smoothing of the bilingual phrase table (Yang and Kirchhoff, 2006).

My approach has some similarity to the FLM: both decompose surface word forms into elements that are generated from unrelated conditional distributions. They differ predominantly along two dimensions: the types of decompositions and conditioning possible, and my use of a particular Bayesian prior for handling smoothing.

In addition to the HPYLM for n-gram language modelling (Teh, 2006), models based on the Pitman-Yor process prior have also been applied to good effect in word segmentation (Goldwater et al., 2006; Mochihashi et al., 2009) and speech recognition (Huang and Renals, 2007; Neubig et al., 2010). The Graphical Pitman-Yor process enables branching back-off paths, which I briefly revisit in §7, and have proved effective in language model domain-adaptation (Wood and Teh, 2009). Here, I extend this general line of inquiry by considering how one might incorporate linguistically informed sub-models into the HPYLM framework.

## 3 Compound Nouns

I focus on compound nouns in this work for two reasons: Firstly, compounding is in general a very productive process, and in some languages (including German, Swedish and Dutch) they are written as single orthographic units. This increases data sparsity and creates significant challenges for NLP systems that use whitespace to identify their elementary modelling units. A proper account of compounds in terms of their component words therefore holds the potential of improving the performance of such systems.

Secondly, there is a clear linguistic intuition to exploit: the morphosyntactic properties of these compounds are often fully determined by the head component within the compound. For example, in "Geburtstagskind" (birthday kid), it is "Kind" that establishes this compound noun as singular neuter, which determine how it would need to agree with verbs, articles and adjectives. In the next section, I propose a model in the suggested framework that encodes this intuition.

The basic structure of German compounds comprises a *head component*, preceded by one or more *modifier components*, with optional *linker elements* between consecutive components (Goldsmith and Reutter, 1998).

### Examples

- The basic form is just the concatenation of two nouns

  Auto + Unfall = Autounfall (car crash)
- Linker elements are sometimes added between components

  Küche + Tisch = Küche<u>n</u>tisch (kitchen table)
- Components can undergo stemming during composition

  Schul<u>e</u> + Hof = Schulhof (schoolyard)
- The process is potentially recursive

  (Geburt + Tag) + Kind = Geburtstag + Kind

  = Geburtstagskind (birthday kid)

The process is not limited to using nouns as components, for example, the numeral in <u>Zwei</u>-Euro-Münze (two Euro coin) or the verb "fahren" (to drive) in <u>Fahr</u>zeug (vehicle). I will treat all these cases the same.

### 3.1 Fluency amid sparsity

Consider the following example from the training corpus used in the subsequent evaluations:

de: Die *Neu*infektionen übersteigen weiterhin die *Behandlungs*bemühungen.

en: *New* infections continue to outpace *treatment* efforts.

The corpus contains numerous other compounds ending in "infektionen" (16) or "bemühungen" (117). A standard word-based n-gram model discriminates among those alternatives using as many independent parameters.

However, we could gauge the approximate syntactic fluency of the sentence almost as well if we ignore the compound modifiers. Collapsing all the variants in this way reduces sparsity and yields better n-gram probability estimates.

To account for the compound modifiers, a simple approach is to use a reverse n-gram language model over compound components, without conditioning on the sentential context. Such a model essentially answers the question, "Given that the word ends in 'infektionen', what modifier(s), if any, are likely to precede it?" The vast majority of nouns will never occur in that position, meaning that the conditional distributions will be sharply peaked.

Figure 1: Intuition for the proposed generative process of a compound word: The context generates the head component, which generates a modifier component, which in turn generates another modifier. (Translation: "with the cable car")

### 3.2 Related Work on Compounds

In machine translation and speech recognition, one approach has been to split compounds as a preprocessing step and merge them back together during postprocessing, while using otherwise unmodified NLP systems. Frequency-based methods have been used for determining how aggressively to split (Koehn and Knight, 2003), since the maximal, linguistically correct segmentation is not necessarily optimal for translation. This gave rise to slight improvements in machine translation evaluations (Koehn et al., 2008), with fine-tuning explored in (Stymne, 2009). Similar ideas have also been employed for speech recognition (Berton et al., 1996) and predictive-text input (Baroni and Matiasek, 2002), where single-token compounds also pose challenges.

## 4 Model Description

### 4.1 HPYLM

Formally speaking, an n-gram model is an $(n-1)$-th order Markov model that approximates the joint probability of a sequence of words $\mathbf{w}$ as

$$P(\mathbf{w}) \approx \prod_{i=1}^{|\mathbf{w}|} P(w_i | w_{i-n+1}, \ldots, w_{i-1}),$$

for which I will occasionally abbreviate a context $[w_i, \ldots, w_j]$ as $\mathbf{u}$. In the HPYLM, the conditional distributions $P(w|\mathbf{u})$ are smoothed by placing Pitman-Yor process priors (PYP) over them. The PYP is defined through its base distribution, and a *strength* $(\theta)$ and *discount* $(d)$ hyperparameter that control its deviation away from its mean (which equals the base distribution).

Let $G_{[u,v]}$ be the PYP-distributed trigram distribution $P(w|u,v)$. The hierarchy arises by using as base distribution for the prior of $G_{[u,v]}$ another PYP-distributed $G_{[v]}$, i.e. the distribution $P(w|v)$. The recursion bottoms out at the unigram distribution $G_{\emptyset}$, which is drawn from a PYP with base distribution equal to the uniform distribution over the vocabulary $\mathcal{W}$. The hyperparameters are tied across all priors with the same context length $|\mathbf{u}|$, and estimated during training.

$$\begin{aligned} G_0 &= \text{Uniform}(|\mathcal{W}|) \\ G_{\emptyset} &\sim PY(d_0, \theta_0, G_0) \\ &\vdots \\ G_{\pi(\mathbf{u})} &\sim PY(d_{|\pi(\mathbf{u})|}, \theta_{|\pi(\mathbf{u})|}, G_{\pi(\pi(\mathbf{u}))}) \\ G_{\mathbf{u}} &\sim PY(d_{|\mathbf{u}|}, \theta_{|\mathbf{u}|}, G_{\pi(\mathbf{u})}) \\ w &\sim G_{\mathbf{u}}, \end{aligned}$$

where $\pi(\mathbf{u})$ truncates the context $\mathbf{u}$ by dropping the left-most word in it.

### 4.2 HPYLM+c

Define a compound word $\tilde{w}$ as a sequence of components $[c_1, \ldots, c_k]$, plus a sentinel symbol \$ marking either the left or the right boundary of the word, depending on the direction of the model. To maintain generality over this choice of direction, let $\Lambda$ be an index set over the positions, such that $c_{\Lambda_1}$ always designates the head component.

Following the motivation in §3.1, I set up the model to generate the head component $c_{\Lambda_1}$ conditioned on the word context $\mathbf{u}$, while the remaining components $\tilde{w} \setminus c_{\Lambda_1}$ are generated by some model $F$, independently of $\mathbf{u}$.

To encode this, I modify the HPYLM in two ways: 1) Replace the support with the reduced vocabulary $\mathcal{M}$, the set of unique components $c$ obtained when segmenting the items in $\mathcal{W}$. 2) Add an additional level of conditional distributions $H_{\mathbf{u}}$ (with $|\mathbf{u}| = n - 1$) where items from $\mathcal{M}$ combine to form the observed surface words:

$$G_{\mathbf{u}} \ldots \text{(as before, except } G_0 = \text{Uniform}(|\mathcal{M}|))$$
$$H_{\mathbf{u}} \sim PY(d_{|\mathbf{u}|}, \theta_{|\mathbf{u}|}, G_{\mathbf{u}} \times F)$$
$$\tilde{w} \sim H_{\mathbf{u}}$$

So the base distribution for the prior of the word n-gram distribution $H_{\mathbf{u}}$ is the product of a distribution $G_{\mathbf{u}}$ over compound heads, given the same context $\mathbf{u}$, and another (n′-gram) language model $F$ over compound modifiers, conditioned on the head component.

Choosing $F$ to be a bigram model (n′=2) yields the following procedure for generating a word:

$$\begin{aligned} & c_{\Lambda_1} \sim G_{\mathbf{u}} \\ & \text{for } i = 2 \text{ to } k \\ & \qquad c_{\Lambda_i} \sim F(\cdot | c_{\Lambda_{i-1}}) \end{aligned}$$

The linguistically motivated choice for conditioning in $F$ is $\Lambda^{\text{ling}} = [k, k-1, \ldots, 1]$ such that $c_{\Lambda_1}$ is the true head component; \$ is drawn from $F(\cdot|c_1)$ and marks the left word boundary.

In order to see if the correct linguistic intuition has any bearing on the model's extrinsic performance, we will also consider the reverse, supposing that the left-most component were actually more important in this task, and letting the remaining components be generated left-to-right. This is expressed by $\Lambda^{\text{inv}} = [1, \ldots, k]$, where \$ this time marks the right word boundary and is drawn from $F(\cdot|c_k)$.

To test whether Kneser-Ney smoothing is indeed sometimes less appropriate, as conjectured earlier, I will also compare the case where $F = F_{KN}$, a KN-smoothed model, with the case where $F = F_{HPYLM}$, another HPYLM.

**Linker Elements** In the preceding definition of compound segmentation, the linker elements do not form part of the vocabulary $\mathcal{M}$. Regarding linker elements as components in their own right would sacrifice important contextual information and disrupt the conditionals $F(\cdot|c_{\Lambda_{i-1}})$. That is, given Küche·n·tisch, we want $P(\text{Küche}|\text{Tisch})$ in the model, but not $P(\text{Küche}|\text{n})$.

But linker elements need to be accounted for somehow to have a well-defined generative model. I follow the pragmatic option of merging any linkers onto the adjacent component – for $\Lambda^{\text{ling}}$ merging happens onto the preceding component, while for $\Lambda^{\text{inv}}$ it is onto the succeeding one. This keeps the 'head' component $c_{\Lambda_1}$ in tact.

More involved strategies could be considered, and it is worth noting that for German the presence and identity of linker elements between $c_i$ and $c_{i+1}$ are in fact governed by the preceding component $c_i$ (Goldsmith and Reutter, 1998).

## 5 Training

For ease of exposition I describe inference with reference to the trigram HPYLM+c model with a bigram HPYLM for $F$, but the general case should be clear.

The model is specified by the latent variables $(G_{[\emptyset]}, G_{[v]}, G_{[u,v]}, H_{[u,v]}, F_\emptyset, F_c)$, where $u, v \in \mathcal{W}$, $c \in \mathcal{M}$, and hyperparameters $\Omega = \{d_i, \theta_i\} \cup \{d'_j, \theta'_j\} \cup \{d''_2, \theta''_2\}$, where $i = 0, 1, 2$, $j = 0, 1$, single primes designate the hyperparameters in $F_{HPYLM}$ and double primes those of $H_{[u,v]}$. We can construct a collapsed Gibbs sampler by marginalising out these latent variables, giving rise to a variant of the hierarchical Chinese Restaurant Process in which it is straightforward to do inference.

**Chinese Restaurant Process** A direct representation of a random variable $G$ drawn from a PYP can be obtained from the so-called stick-breaking construction. But the more indirect representation by means of the Chinese Restaurant Process (CRP) (Pitman, 2002) is more suitable here since it relates to distributions over items drawn from such a $G$. This fits the current setting, where words $w$ are being drawn from a PYP-distributed $G$.

Imagine that a corpus is created in two phases: Firstly, a sequence of blank tokens $x_i$ is instantiated, and in a second phase lexical identities $w_i$ are assigned to these tokens, giving rise to the observed corpus. In the CRP metaphor , the sequence of tokens $x_i$ are equated with a sequence of customers that enter a restaurant one-by-one to be seated at one of an infinite number of tables. When a customer sits at an unoccupied table $k$, they order a dish $\phi_k$ for the table, but customers joining an occupied table have to dine on the dish already served there. The dish $\phi_i$ that each customer eats is equated to the lexical identity $w_i$ of the corresponding token, and the way in which tables and dishes are chosen give rise to the characteristic properties of the CRP:

More formally, let $x_1, x_2, \ldots$ be draws from $G$, while $t$ is the number of occupied tables, $c$ the number of customers in the restaurant, and $c_k$ the number of customers at the $k$-th table. Conditioned on preceding customers $x_1, \ldots, x_{i-1}$ and their arrangement, the $i$-th customer sits at table $k = k'$ according to the following probabilities:

$$\Pr(k'|\ldots) \propto \begin{cases} c_{k'} - d & \text{occupied table } k' \\ \theta + dt & \text{unoccupied table } t+1 \end{cases}$$

Ordering a dish for a new table corresponds to drawing a value $\phi_k$ from the base distribution $G_0$, and it is perfectly acceptable to serve the same kind of dish at multiple tables.

Some characteristic behaviour of the CRP can be observed easily from this description: 1) As more customers join a table, that table becomes a more likely choice for future customers too. 2) Regardless of how many customers there are, there is always a non-zero probability of joining an unoccupied table, and this probability also depends on the number of total tables.

The dish draws can be seen as backing off to the underlying base distribution $G_0$, an important consideration in the context of the hierarchical variant of the process explained shortly. Note that the strength and discount parameters control the extent to which new dishes are drawn, and thus the extent of reliance on the base distribution.

The predictive probability of a word $w$ given a seating arrangement is given by

$$\Pr(w|\ldots) \propto c_w - dt_w + (\theta + dt)G_0(w)$$

In smoothing terminology, the first term can be interpreted as applying a discount of $dt_w$ to the observed count $c_w$ of $w$; the amount of discount therefore depends on the prevalence of the word (via $t_w$). This is one significant way in which the PYP/CRP gives more nuanced smoothing than modified Kneser-Ney, which only uses four different discount levels (Chen and Goodman, 1998). Similarly, if the seating dynamics are constrained such that each dish is only served once ($t_w = 1$ for any $w$), a single discount level is affected, establishing direct correspondence to original interpolated Kneser-Ney smoothing (Teh, 2006).

**Hierarchical CRP** When the prior of $G_{\mathbf{u}}$ has a base distribution $G_{\pi(\mathbf{u})}$ that is itself PYP-distributed, as in the HPYLM, the restaurant metaphor changes slightly. In general, each node in the hierarchy has an associated restaurant. Whenever a new table is opened in some restaurant $R$, another customer is plucked out of thin air and sent to join the parent restaurant pa$(R)$. This induces a consistency constraint over the hierarchy: the number of tables $t_w$ in restaurant $R$ must equal the number of customers $c_w$ in its parent pa$(R)$.

In the proposed HPYLM+c model using $F_{HPYLM}$, there is a further constraint of a similar nature: When a new table is opened and serves dish $\phi = \tilde{w}$ in the trigram restaurant for $H_{[u,v]}$, a customer $c_{\Lambda_1}$ is sent to the corresponding bigram restaurant for $G_{[u,v]}$, *and* customers $c_{\Lambda_{2:k}}$,\$ are sent to the restaurants for $F_{c'}$, for contexts $c' = c_{\Lambda_{1:k-1}}$. This latter requirement is novel here compared to the hierarchical CRP used to realise the original HPYLM.

**Sampling** Although the CRP allows us to replace the priors with seating arrangements $S$, those seating arrangements are simply latent variables that need to be integrated out to get a true predictive probability of a word:

$$p(w|\mathcal{D}) = \int_{S,\Omega} p(w|S,\Omega)p(S,\Omega|\mathcal{D}),$$

where $\mathcal{D}$ is the training data and, as before, $\Omega$ are the parameters. This integral can be approximated by averaging over $m$ posterior samples $(S, \Omega)$ generated using Markov chain Monte Carlo methods. The simple form of the conditionals in the CRP allows us to do a Gibbs update whereby the table index $k$ of a customer is resampled conditioned on all the other variables. Sampling a new seating arrangement $S$ for the trigram HPYLM+c thus corresponds to visiting each customer in the restaurants for $H_{[u,v]}$, removing them while cascading as necessary to observe the consistency across the hierarchy, and seating them anew at some table $k'$.

In the absence of any strong intuitions about appropriate values for the hyperparameters, I place vague priors over them and use slice sampling[1] (Neal, 2003) to update their values during generation of the posterior samples:

$$d \sim \text{Beta}(1,1) \qquad \theta \sim \text{Gamma}(1,1)$$

Lastly, I make the further approximation of $m = 1$, i.e. predictive probabilities are informed by a single posterior sample $(S, \Omega)$.

## 6 Experiments

The aim of the experiments reported here is to test whether the richer account of compounds in the proposed language models has positive effects on the predictability of unseen text and the generation of better translations.

### 6.1 Methods

**Data and Tools** Standard data preprocessing steps included normalising punctuation, tokenising and lowercasing all words. All data sets are from the WMT11 shared-task.[2]. The full English-German bitext was filtered to exclude sentences longer than 50, resulting in 1.7 million parallel sentences; word alignments were inferred from this using the Berkeley Aligner (Liang et al., 2006) and used as basis from which to extract a Hiero-style synchronous CFG (Chiang, 2007).

The weights of the log-linear translation models were tuned towards the BLEU metric on development data using `cdec`'s (Dyer et al., 2010) implementation of MERT (Och, 2003). For this, the set `news-test2008` (2051 sentences) was used, while final case-insensitive BLEU scores are measured on the official test set `newstest2011` (3003 sentences).

All language models were trained on the target side of the preprocessed bitext containing 38 million tokens, and tested on all the German development data (i.e. `news-test2008,9,10`).

**Compound segmentation** To construct a segmentation dictionary, I used the 1-best segmentations from a supervised MaxEnt compound splitter (Dyer, 2009) run on all token types in bitext. In addition, word-internal hyphens were also taken as segmentation points. Finally, linker elements were merged onto components as discussed in §4.2. Any token that is split into more than one part by this procedure is regarded as a compound. The effect of the individual steps is summarised in Table 1.

| | # Types | Example |
|---|---|---|
| None | 350998 | Geburtstagskind |
| pre-merge | 201328 | Geburtstag·kind |
| merge, $\Lambda^{\text{ling}}$ | 150980 | Geburtstags·kind |
| merge, $\Lambda^{\text{inv}}$ | 162722 | Geburtstag·skind |

Table 1: Effect of segmentation on vocabulary size.

**Metrics** For intrinsic evaluation of language models, perplexity is a common metric. Given a trained model $q$, the perplexity over the words $\tau$ in unseen test set $T$ is $\exp\left(-\frac{1}{|T|}\sum_\tau \ln(q(\tau))\right)$.

One convenience of this per-word perplexity is that it can be compared consistently across different test sets regardless of their lengths; its neat interpretation is another: a model that achieves a perplexity of $\eta$ on a test set is on average $\eta$-ways confused about each word. Less confusion and therefore lower test set perplexity is indicative of a better model. This allows different models to be compared relative to the same test set.

The exponent above can be regarded as an approximation of the cross-entropy between the model $q$ and a hypothetical model $p$ from which both the training and test set were putatively generated. It is sometimes convenient to use this as an alternative measure.

But a language model only really becomes useful when it allows some extrinsic task to be executed better. When that extrinsic task is machine translation, the translation quality can be assessed to see if one language model aids it more than another. The obligatory metric for evaluating machine translation quality is BLEU (Papineni et al., 2001), a precision based metric that measures how close the machine output is to a known correct translation (the reference sentences in the test set). Higher precision means the translation system is getting more phrases right.

Better language model perplexities sometimes lead to improvements in translation quality, but it is not guaranteed. Moreover, even when real translation improvements are obtained, they are

[1] Mark Johnson's implementation, `http://www.cog.brown.edu/~mj/Software.htm`

[2] `http://www.statmt.org/wmt11/`

| | PPL | c-Cross-ent. |
|---|---|---|
| mKN | 441.32 | **0.1981** |
| HPYLM | 429.17 | 0.1994 |
| $F_{KN}$ $\Lambda^{\text{ling}}$ | 432.95 | 0.2028 |
| $F_{KN}$ $\Lambda^{\text{inv}}$ | 446.84 | 0.2125 |
| $F_{HPYLM}$ $\Lambda^{\text{ling}}$ | **421.63** | 0.1987 |
| $F_{HPYLM}$ $\Lambda^{\text{inv}}$ | 435.79 | 0.2079 |

Table 2: Monolingual evaluation results. The second column shows perplexity measured all WMT11 German development data (7065 sentences). At the word level, all are trigram models, while $F$ are bigram models using the specified segmentation scheme. The third column has test cross-entropies measured only on the 6099 compounds in the test set (given their contexts ).

not guaranteed to be noticeable in the BLEU score, especially when targeting an arguably narrow phenomenon like compounding.

| | BLEU |
|---|---|
| mKN | 13.11 |
| HPYLM | 13.20 |
| $F_{HPYLM}$, $\Lambda^{\text{ling}}$ | 13.24 |
| $F_{HPYLM}$, $\Lambda^{\text{inv}}$ | **13.32** |

Table 3: Translation results, BLEU (1-ref), 3003 test sentences. Trigram language models, no count pruning, no "unknown word" token.

| | P / R / F |
|---|---|
| mKN | 22.0 / 17.3 / 19.4 |
| HPYLM | 21.0 / 17.8 / 19.3 |
| $F_{HPYLM}$, $\Lambda^{\text{ling}}$ | 23.6 / 17.3 / **19.9** |
| $F_{HPYLM}$, $\Lambda^{\text{inv}}$ | 24.1 / 16.5 / 19.6 |

Table 4: Precision, Recall and F-score of compound translations, relative to reference set (72661 tokens, of which 2649 are compounds).

### 6.2 Main Results

For the monolingual evaluation, I used an interpolated, modified Kneser-Ney model (mKN) and an HPYLM as baselines. It has been shown for other languages that HPYLM tends to outperform mKN (Okita and Way, 2010), but I am not aware of this result being demonstrated on German before, as I do in Table 2.

The main model of interest is HPYLM+c using the $\Lambda^{\text{ling}}$ segmentation and a model $F_{HPYLM}$ over modifiers; this model achieves the lowest perplexity, 4.4% lower than the mKN baseline.

Next, note that using $F_{KN}$ to handle the modifiers does worse than $F_{HPYLM}$, confirming our expectation that KN is less appropriate for that task, although it still does better than the original mKN baseline.

The models that use the linguistically implausible segmentation scheme $\Lambda^{\text{inv}}$ both fare worse than their counterparts that use the sensible scheme, but of all tested models only $F_{KN}$ & $\Lambda^{\text{inv}}$ fails to beat the mKN baseline. This suggests that in some sense having *any* account whatsoever of compound formation tends to have a beneficial effect on this test set – the richer statistics due to a smaller vocabulary could be sufficient to explain this – but to get the most out of it one needs the superior smoothing over modifiers (provided by $F_{HPYLM}$) and adherence to linguistic intuition (via $\Lambda^{\text{ling}}$).

As for the translation experiments, the relative qualitative performance of the two baseline language models carries over to the BLEU score (HPYLM does 0.09 points better than KN), and is further improved upon slightly by using two variants of HPYLM+c (Table 3).

### 6.3 Analysis

To get a better idea of how the extended models employ the increased expressiveness, I calculated the cross-entropy over only the compound words in the monolingual test set (second column of Table 2). Among the HPYLM+c variants, we see that their performance on compounds only is consistent with their performance (relative to each other) on the whole corpus. This implies that the differences in whole-corpus perplexities are at least in part due to their different levels of adeptness at handling compounds, as opposed to some fluke event.

It is, however, somewhat surprising to observe that HPYLM+c do not achieve a lower compound cross-entropy than the mKN baseline, as it suggests that HPYLM+c's perplexity reductions compared to mKN arise in part from something other than compound handling, which is their whole point.

This discrepancy could be related to the fairness of this direct comparison of models that ultimately model different sets of things: According to the generative process of HPYLM+c (§4), there is no limit on the number of components in a compound: in theory, an arbitrary number of components $c \in \mathcal{M}$ can combine to form a word. HPYLM+c is thus defined over a countably infinite set of words, thereby reserving some probability mass for items that will never be realised in any corpus, whereas the baseline models are defined only over the finite set $\mathcal{W}$. These direct comparisons are thus lightly skewed in favour of the baselines. This bolsters confidence in the perplexity reductions presented in the previous section, but the skew may afflict compounds more starkly, leading to the slight discrepancy observed in the compound cross-entropies. What matters more is the performance among the HPYLM+c variants, since they are directly comparable.

To home in still further on the compound modelling, I selected those compounds for which HPYLM+c ($F_{HPYLM}, \Lambda^{\text{ling}}$) does best/worst in terms of the probabilities assigned, compared to the mKN baseline (see Table 5). One pattern that emerges is that the "top" compounds mostly consist of components that are likely to be quite common, and that this improves estimates both for n-grams that are very rare (the singleton "senkungen der treibhausgasemmissionen" = *decreases in green house gas emissions*) or relatively common (158, "der hauptstadt" = *of the capital*).

| **n-gram** | **Δ** | **C** |
|---:|---|---|
| gesichts·punkten | 0.064 | 335 |
| 700 milliarden us-·dollar | 0.021 | 2 |
| s. der treibhausgas·emissionen | 0.018 | 1 |
| r. der treibhausgas·emissionen | 0.011 | 3 |
| ministerium für land·wirtschaft | 0.009 | 11 |
| bildungs·niveaus | 0.009 | 14 |
| newt ging·rich* | -0.257 | 2 |
| nouri al-·maliki* | -0.257 | 3 |
| klerikers moqtada al-·sadr* | -0.258 | 1 |
| nuri al-·maliki* | -0.337 | 3 |
| sankt peters·burg* | -0.413 | 35 |
| nächtlichem flug·lärm | -0.454 | 2 |

Table 5: Compound n-grams in the test set for which the absolute difference $\Delta = P_{\text{HPYLM+c}} - P_{\text{mKN}}$ is greatest. **C** is n-gram count in the training data. Asterisks denote words that are not compounds, linguistically speaking. Abbrevs: r. = reduktionen, s.= senkungen

On the other hand, the "bottom" compounds are mostly ones whose components will be uncommon; in fact, many of them are not truly compounds but artefacts of the somewhat greedy segmentation procedure I used. Alternative procedures will be tested in future work.

Since the BLEU scores do not reveal much about the new language models' effect on compound translation, I also calculated compound-specific accuracies, using precision, recall and F-score (Table 4). Here, the precision for a single sentence would be 100% if all the compounds in the output sentence occur in the reference translation. Compared to the baselines, the compound precision goes up noticeably under the HPYLM+c models used in translation, without sacrificing on recall. This suggests that these models are helping to weed out incorrectly hypothesised compounds.

### 6.4 Caveats

All results are based on single runs and are therefore not entirely robust. In particular, MERT tuning of the translation model is known to introduce significant variance in translation performance across different runs, and the small differences in BLEU scores reported in Table 3 are very likely to lie in that region.

Markov chain convergence also needs further attention. In absence of complex latent structure (for the dishes), the chain should mix fairly quickly, and as attested by Figure 2 it 'converges' with respect to the test metric after about 20 samples, although the log posterior (not shown) had not converged after 40. The use of a single posterior sample could also be having a negative effect on results.

## 7 Future Directions

The first goal will be to get more robust experimental results, and to scale up to 4-gram models estimated on all the available monolingual training data. If good performance can be demonstrated under those conditions, this general approach could pass as a viable alternative to the current Kneser-Ney dominated state-of-the art setup in MT.

Much of the power of the HPYLM+c model has not been exploited in this evaluation, in particular its ability to score unseen compounds consisting of known components. This feature was

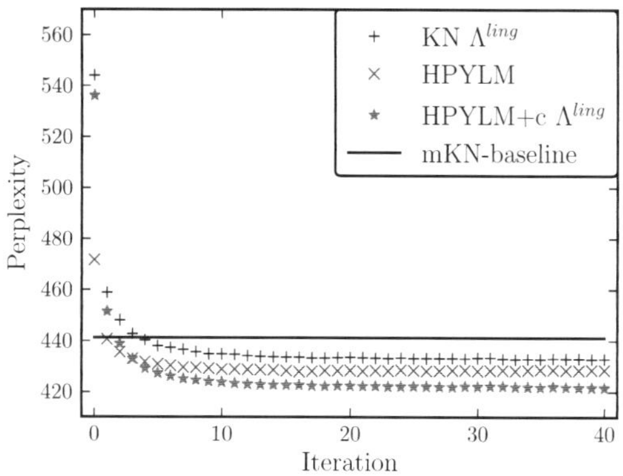


Figure 2: Convergence of test set perplexities.

not active in these evaluations, mostly due to the current phase of implementation. A second area of focus is thus to modify the decoder to generate such unseen compounds in translation hypotheses. Given the current low compound recall rates, this could greatly benefit translation quality. An informal analysis of the reference translations in the bilingual test set showed that 991 of the 1406 out-of-vocabulary compounds (out of 2692 OOVs in total) fall into this category of unseen-but-recognisable compounds.

Ultimately the idea is to apply this modelling approach to other linguistic phenomena as well. In particular, the objective is to model instances of concatenative morphology beyond compounding, with the aim of improving translation into morphologically rich languages. Complex agreement patterns could be captured by conditioning functional morphemes in the target word on morphemes in the n-gram context, or by stemming context words during back-off. Such additional back-off paths can be readily encoded in the Graphical Pitman-Yor process (Wood and Teh, 2009).

These more complex models may require longer to train. To this end, I intend to use the single table per dish approximation (§5) to reduce training to a single deterministic pass through the data, conjecturing that this will have little effect on extrinsic performance.

## 8 Summary

I have argued for further explorations into the use of a family of hierarchical Bayesian models for targeting linguistic phenomena that may not be captured well by standard n-gram language models. To ground this investigation, I focused on German compounds and showed how these models are an appropriate vehicle for encoding prior linguistic intuitions about such compounds. The proposed generative model beats the popular modified Kneser-Ney model in monolingual evaluations, and preliminarily achieves small improvements in translation from English into German. In this translation task, single-token German compounds traditionally pose challenges to translation systems, and preliminary results show a small increase in the F-score accuracy of compounds in the translation output. Finally, I have outlined the intended steps for expanding this line of inquiry into other related linguistic phenomena and for adapting a translation system to get optimal value out of such improved language models.

## Acknowledgements

Thanks goes to my supervisor, Phil Blunsom, for continued support and advice; to Chris Dyer for suggesting the focus on German compounds and supplying a freshly trained compound splitter; to the Rhodes Trust for financial support; and to the anonymous reviewers for their helpful feedback.

## References


Marco Baroni and Johannes Matiasek. 2002. Predicting the components of German nominal compounds. In *ECAI*, pages 470–474.

Andre Berton, Pablo Fetter, and Peter Regel-Brietzmann. 1996. Compound Words in Large-Vocabulary German Speech Recognition Systems. In *Proceedings of Fourth International Conference on Spoken Language Processing. ICSLP '96*, volume 2, pages 1165–1168. IEEE.

Jeff A Bilmes and Katrin Kirchhoff. 2003. Factored language models and generalized parallel backoff. In *Proceedings of NAACL-HLT (short papers)*, pages 4–6, Stroudsburg, PA, USA. Association for Computational Linguistics.

Stanley F Chen and Joshua Goodman. 1998. An Empirical Study of Smoothing Techniques for Language Modeling. Technical report.

David Chiang. 2007. Hierarchical Phrase-Based Translation. *Computational Linguistics*, 33(2):201–228, June.

Chris Dyer, Adam Lopez, Juri Ganitkevitch, Johnathan Weese, Ferhan Ture, Phil Blunsom, Hendra Setiawan, Vladimir Eidelman, and Philip Resnik. 2010. cdec: A Decoder, Alignment, and Learning framework for finite-state and context-free translation models. In *Proceedings of the Association for Computational Linguistics (Demonstration session)*, pages 7–12, Uppsala, Sweden. Association for Computational Linguistics.

Chris Dyer. 2009. Using a maximum entropy model to build segmentation lattices for MT. In *Proceedings of NAACL*, pages 406–414. Association for Computational Linguistics.

John Goldsmith and Tom Reutter. 1998. Automatic Collection and Analysis of German Compounds. In F. Busa F. et al., editor, *The Computational Treatment of Nominals*, pages 61–69. Universite de Montreal, Canada.

Sharon Goldwater, Thomas L. Griffiths, and Mark Johnson. 2006. Interpolating Between Types and Tokens by Estimating Power-Law Generators. In *Advances in Neural Information Processing Systems, Volume 18*.

Songfang Huang and Steve Renals. 2007. Hierarchical Pitman-Yor Language Models For ASR in Meetings. *IEEE ASRU*, pages 124–129.

Songfang Huang and Steve Renals. 2009. A parallel training algorithm for hierarchical Pitman-Yor process language models. In *Proceedings of Interspeech*, volume 9, pages 2695–2698.

Reinhard Kneser and Hermann Ney. 1995. Improved backing-off for m-gram language modelling. In *Proceedings of the IEEE International Conference on Acoustics, Speech and SIgnal Processing*, pages 181–184.

Philipp Koehn and Kevin Knight. 2003. Empirical Methods for Compound Splitting. In *Proceedings of EACL*, pages 187–193. Association for Computational Linguistics.

Philipp Koehn, Abhishek Arun, and Hieu Hoang. 2008. Towards better Machine Translation Quality for the German – English Language Pairs. In *Third Workshop on Statistical Machine Translation*, number June, pages 139–142. Association for Computational Linguistics.

Percy Liang, Ben Taskar, and Dan Klein. 2006. Alignment by Agreement. In *Proceedings of the Human Language Technology Conference of the NAACL, Main Conference*, pages 104–111, New York City, USA, June. Association for Computational Linguistics.

Daichi Mochihashi, Takeshi Yamada, and Naonori Ueda. 2009. Bayesian unsupervised word segmentation with nested Pitman-Yor language modeling. In *Proceedings of the Joint Conference of the 47th Annual Meeting of the ACL and the 4th International Joint Conference on Natural Language Processing of the AFNLP: Volume 1 - ACL-IJCNLP '09*, pages 100–108, Suntec, Singapore. Association for Computational Linguistics.

Radford M Neal. 2003. Slice Sampling. *The Annals of Statistics*, 31(3):705–741.

Graham Neubig, Masato Mimura, Shinsuke Mori, and Tatsuya Kawahara. 2010. Learning a Language Model from Continuous Speech. In *Interspeech*, pages 1053–1056, Chiba, Japan.

Franz Josef Och. 2003. Minimum Error Rate Training in Statistical Machine Translation. In *Proceedings of ACL*, pages 160–167.

Tsuyoshi Okita and Andy Way. 2010. Hierarchical Pitman-Yor Language Model for Machine Translation. *Proceedings of the International Conference on Asian Language Processing*, pages 245–248.

Kishore Papineni, Salim Roukos, Todd Ward, Weijing Zhu, Thomas J Watson, and Yorktown Heights. 2001. Bleu: A Method for Automatic Evaluation of Machine Translation. Technical report, IBM.

J Pitman and M. Yor. 1997. The two-parameter Poisson-Dirichlet distribution derived from a stable subordinator. *The Annals of Probability*, 25:855–900.

J. Pitman. 2002. Combinatorial stochastic processes. Technical report, Department of Statistics, University of California at Berkeley.

Sara Stymne. 2009. A comparison of merging strategies for translation of German compounds. *Proceedings of the 12th Conference of the European Chapter of the Association for Computational Linguistics: Student Research Workshop*, pages 61–69.

Yee Whye Teh. 2006. A hierarchical Bayesian language model based on Pitman-Yor processes. In *Proceedings of the 21st International Conference on Computational Linguistics and the 44th annual meeting of the ACL*, pages 985–992. Association for Computational Linguistics.

Frank Wood and Yee Whye Teh. 2009. A Hierarchical Nonparametric Bayesian Approach to Statistical Language Model Domain Adaptation. In *Proceedings of the 12th International Conference on Artificial Intelligence and Statistics (AISTATS)*, pages 607–614, Clearwater Beach, Florida, USA.

Mei Yang and Katrin Kirchhoff. 2006. Phrase-based Backoff Models for Machine Translation of Highly Inflected Languages. In *Proceedings of the EACL*, pages 41–48.

# Mining Co-Occurrence Matrices for SO-PMI Paradigm Word Candidates

**Aleksander Wawer**
Institute of Computer Science, Polish Academy of Science
ul. Jana Kazimierza 5
01-248 Warszawa, Poland
axw@ipipan.waw.pl

## Abstract

This paper is focused on one aspect of SO-PMI, an unsupervised approach to sentiment vocabulary acquisition proposed by Turney (Turney and Littman, 2003). The method, originally applied and evaluated for English, is often used in bootstrapping sentiment lexicons for European languages where no such resources typically exist. In general, SO-PMI values are computed from word co-occurrence frequencies in the neighbourhoods of two small sets of paradigm words. The goal of this work is to investigate how lexeme selection affects the quality of obtained sentiment estimations. This has been achieved by comparing ad hoc random lexeme selection with two alternative heuristics, based on clustering and SVD decomposition of a word co-occurrence matrix, demonstrating superiority of the latter methods. The work can be also interpreted as sensitivity analysis on SO-PMI with regard to paradigm word selection. The experiments were carried out for Polish.

## 1 Introduction

This paper seeks to improve one of the main methods of unsupervised lexeme sentiment polarity assignment. The method, introduced by (Turney and Littman, 2003), is described in more detail in Section 2. It relies on two sets of paradigm words, positive and negative, which determine the polarity of unseen words.

The method is resource lean and therefore often used in languages other than English. Recent examples include Japanese (Wang and Araki, 2007) and German (Remus et al., 2006).

Unfortunately, the selection of paradigm words rarely receives sufficient attention and is typically done in an *ad hoc* manner. One notable example of manual paradigm word selection method was presented in (Read and Carroll, 2009).

In this context, an interesting variation of the semantic orientation–pointwise mutual information (SO-PMI) algorithm for Japanese was suggested by (Wang and Araki, 2007). Authors, motivated by excessive leaning toward positive opinions, proposed to modify the algorithm by introducing balancing factor and detecting neutral expressions. As will be demonstrated, this problem can be addressed by proper selection of paradigm pairs.

One not entirely realistic, but nevertheless interesting theoretical possibility is to pick pairs of opposing adjectives with the highest loadings identified in Osgood's experiments on semantic differential (Osgood et al., 1967). In the experiments, respondents were presented with a noun and asked to choose its appropriate position on a scale between two bipolar adjectives (for example: *adequate-inadequate*, *valuable-worthless*, *hot-cold*). Factor analysis of the results revealed three distinctive factors, called Osgood dimensions. The first of the dimensions, often considered synonymous with the notion of *sentiment*, was called Evaluative because its foundational adjective pair (one with the highest loading) is *good-bad*.

The first problem with using adjective pairs as exemplary for word co-occurrence distributions on the basis of their loadings, is the fact that factor loadings as measured by Osgood et al. are not necessarily reflected in word frequency phenomena.

The second problem is translation: an adjective pair, central in English, may not be as strongly associated with a dimension (here: Evaluative) in other languages and cultures.

The approach we suggest in this paper assumes a latent structure behind word co-occurrence frequencies. The structure may be seen as a mixture of latent variables of unknown distributions that drives word selection. Some of the variables are more likely to produce certain types of highly evaluative words (words with high sentiment scores). We do not attempt to model the structure in a generative way as in for example probabilistic latent semantic analysis (PLSA) or latent Dirichlet allocation (LDA). A generative approximation is not feasible when using corpora such as the balanced, 300-million version of the National Corpus of Polish (NKJP) (Przepiórkowski et al., 2008; Przepiórkowski et al., 2012) [1] applied in the experiments described in the next sections, which does not enable creating a word-document matrix and organizing word occurrences by documents or narrowly specified topics.

Therefore, we propose different techniques. We begin with a symmetric matrix of word co-occurences and attempt to discover as much of its structure as possible using two well established techniques: Singular Value Decomposition and clustering. The discovered structures are then used to optimize the selection of words for paradigm sets used in SO-PMI.

The paper is organized as follows. In Section 2 we define the SO-PMI measure and briefly formulate the problem. Section 3 describes obtaining the set of sentiment word candidates, which are then used to generate a symmetric co-occurence matrix as outlined in Section 4. Section 5 delineates the details of human word scoring, which serves as a basis for evaluations in 9. Sections 6, 7 and 8 describe three distinct approaches to paradigm sets generation.

## 2 Problem Statement. SO-PMI

When creating a sentiment lexicon, the strength of association between candidate words and each of the two polar classes (positive and negative, for instance) can be calculated using several measures. Perhaps most popular of them, employed in this experiment after (Turney and Littman, 2003) and (Grefenstette et al., 2006) is Pointwise Mutual Information (PMI). The Pointwise Mutual Information (PMI) between two words, *w1* and *w2*, is defined as:

$$\mathrm{PMI}(w1, w2) = \log_2 \left( \frac{p(w1 \& w2)}{p(w1)p(w2)} \right)$$

where p(w1 & w2) is the probability of co-occurrence of (w1) and (w2). For the task of assigning evaluative polarity, it is computed as number of co-occurrences of candidate words with each of the paradigm positive and negative words, denoted as $pw$ and $nw$. Optimal selection of these two sets of words is the subject of this paper.

Once the words are known, the semantic orientation PMI (SO-PMI) of each candidate word $c$ can be computed as:

$$\text{SO-PMI}(c) =$$
$$= \sum_{pw \in PW} \mathrm{PMI}(c, pw) - \sum_{nw \in NW} \mathrm{PMI}(c, nw)$$

The equation above demonstrates that optimization of both word lists, $pw$ and $nw$, is of crucial importance for the performance of SO-PMI.

## 3 Generating Sentiment Word Candidates

This section describes the acquisition of sentiment word candidates. The method we followed could be substituted by any other technique which results in a set of highly sentimental lexemes, possibly of varying unknown polarity and strength. A similar experiment for English has been described by (Grefenstette et al., 2006).

The procedure can be described as follows. In the first step, a set of semi-manually defined lexical patterns is submitted to a search engine to find candidates for evaluatively charged terms. Then, the downloaded corpus is analyzed for pattern continuations – lexemes immediately following pattern matches, which are likely to be candidates for sentiment words. In the last step, candidate terms selected this way are tested for their sentiment strength and polarity (in other words, how positive or negative are the conotations). In original experiment described in the cited paper, words were evaluated using the SO-PMI technique.

[1] `http://www.nkjp.pl/index.php?page=0&lang=1`

The purpose of using extraction patterns is to select candidates for evaluative words. In this experiment, 112 patterns have been created by generating all combinations of elements from two manually prepared sets[2], **A** and **B**:

- **A:** *[0] wydawać się, [1] wydawał się, [2] wydawała się, [3] czuć się, [4] czułem się, [5] czułam się, [6] czułem, [7] być* [3]

- **B:** *[0] nie dość, [1] niewystarczająco, [2] niedostatecznie, [3] za mało, [4] prawie, [5] niemal, [6] tak, [7] taki, [8] zbyt, [9] zbytnio, [10] za bardzo, [11] przesadnie, [12] nadmiernie, [13] szczególnie* [4]

Each pattern (a combination of A and B) has been wrapped with double quotes ("**A B**") and submitted to Google to narrow the results to texts with exact phrases. The Web crawl yielded 17657 web pages, stripped from HTML and other web tags to filter out non-textual content. Two patterns are grammatically incorrect due to gender disagreement, namely *wydawała się taki* and *czułam się taki* [5], thus did not generate any results.

The corpus of 17657 web pages has been analyzed using Spejd[6], originally a tool for partial parsing and rule-based morphosyntactic disambiguation, adapted in the context of this work for the purpose of finding pattern continuations. Again, 112 patterns were constructed by generating all combinations of elements from the two sets, **A** and **B** above. Spejd rules were written as "**A B** *" where the wildcard can be either an adjective or an adverb.

Parsing the web pages using the 112 patterns resulted in acquiring 1325 distinct base word forms (lexemes) recognized by the morphologic analyser and related dictionaries. This list is subsequently used for generating the co-occurrence matrix as delineated in the next Section and for selecting paradigm words.

## 4 Word Co-Occurrence Matrix

Each word (base form) from the list was sought in the balanced, 300 million segments[7] version of the National Corpus of Polish (NKJP). For each row $i$ and column $j$ of the co-occurrence matrix $m$, its value was computed as follows:

$$m_{ij} = \frac{f_{ij}}{f_i f_j}$$

where $f_{ij}$ denotes the number of co-occurences of word $i$ within the window of 20 segments left and right with word $j$, $f_i$ and $f_j$ denote the total numbers of occurrences of each word. The selection of a window of 20 follows the choice in (Turney and Littman, 2003).

This design has been found optimal after a number of experiments with the singular value decomposition (SVD) technique described further. Without the denominator part, decompositions are heavily biased by word frequency. In this defnition, the matrix resembles the $PMI$ form in (Turney and Pantel, 2010), however we found that the logarithm transformation flattens the eigenvalue distribution and is not really necessary.

If the distributions of words $i$ and $j$ are statistically independent, then by the defnition of independence $f_i f_j = f_{ij}$. The product $f_i f_j$ is what we would expect for $f_{ij}$, if $i$ occurs in the contexts of $j$ by the matter of a random chance. The opposing situation happens when there exists a relationship between $i$ and $j$, for instance when both words are generated by the same latent topic variable, and we expect $f_{ij}$ to be larger than in the case of independency.

## 5 Evaluating Word Candidates

In order to evaluate combinations of paradigm words, one needs to compare the computed SO-PMI scores against a human made scoring. Ideally, such a scoring should not only inform about polarity (indication whether a word is positive or negative), but also about association strength (the degree of positivity or negativity). Reliable and

[2] Terms are translations of words listed in (Grefenstette et al., 2006). Many of the expressions denote either excess or deficiency, as for example *not enough* or *too much*.

[3] English translations (morphosyntactic tags in parentheses): [0] *seem to* (inf), [1] *seemed to* (sg,pri,perf,m), [2] *seemed to* (sg,pri,perf,f), [3] *feel* (inf), [4] *felt* (sg,pri,perf,m), [5] *felt* (sg,pri,perf,f), [7] *to be* (inf)

[4] items [0-3] are various ways of expressing *not enough*, items [4-5] *almost*, items [6-7] *such*, items [8-12] *too much*, item [13] *especially*

[5] *seemed(f) so(m)* and *felt(f) so(m)*

[6] `http://nlp.ipipan.waw.pl/Spejd/` (Przepiórkowski and Buczyński, 2007)

[7] A segment usually corresponds to a word. Segments are not longer than orthographic words, but sometimes shorter. See `http://nkjp.pl/poliqarp/help/ense1.html#x2-10001` for a detailed discussion

valid measurement of word associations on a multipoint scale is not easy: the inter rater agreement is likely to decrease with the growing complexity of the scale.

Therefore, we decided that each lexeme was independently scored by two humans using a five point scale. Extreme values denoted **very** negative or positive words, the central value denoted neutral words and remaining intermediate values were interpreted as **somehow** positive or negative. Discrepancies between raters were solved by arithmetic means of conflicting scores rather than introducing the third human (often called the Golden Annotator) to select one value of the two. Consequently, the 5-point scale extended to 10 points.

Human word scores were used in evaluations of methods described in forthcoming sections.

## 6 Random Selection

The baseline method to compare against is to select lexemes in a random fashion. In order to ensure highest possible performance of the method, lexemes were selected only from those with at least one extreme human score (very positive or very negative) and at least 500 occurrences in the corpus. The last condition renders this method slightly favourable because in the case of SVD, in many eigenvectors the highly loaded terms were not as frequent and had to be selected despite relative rarity.

## 7 SVD

The word co-occurrence matrix $m$ (1325x1325) was the subject of singular value decomposition (SVD), a well-known matrix factorization technique which decomposes a matrix $A$ into three matrices:

$$A = U\Sigma V^T$$

where $\Sigma$ is a matrix whose diagonals are the singular values of $A$, $U$ and $V$ are left and right eigenvectors matrices.

The usage of SVD decompositions has a long and successful history of applications in extracting meaning from word frequencies in word-document matrices, as for example the well established algorithm of latent semantic indexing (LSI). More recently, the usability of analyzing the structure of language via spectral analysis of co-occurrence matrices was demonstrated by studies such as (Mukherjee et al., 2009). The focus was on phonology with the intention to discover principles governing consonant inventories and quantify their importance. Our work, as we believe, is the first to apply SVD in the context of co-occurrence matrices and SO-PMI.

We suspect that the SVD technique can be helpful by selecting lexemes that represent certain amounts of latent co-occurrence structure. Furthermore, the fact that 20 eigenvalues constitutes approximately half of the norm of the spectrum (Horn and Johnson, 1990), as on Table 1, suggests that there may exist a small number of organizing principles which could be potentially helpful to improve the selection of lexemes into paradigm sets.

| | $c$ | $m$ |
|---|---|---|
| 10 | 0.728 | 0.410 |
| 20 | 0.797 | 0.498 |
| 100 | 0.924 | 0.720 |

Table 1: Frobenius norm of the spectrum for 10, 20 and 100 first eigenvalues.

Table 1 depicts also the problem of frequency bias, stronger in case of 10 and 20 eigenvalues than for 100. The values were computed for two matrices: $c$ contains only co-occurrence frequencies and $m$ is the matrix described in section 4. Figure 1 plots the eigenvalue spectrum restricted to the first 100 values.

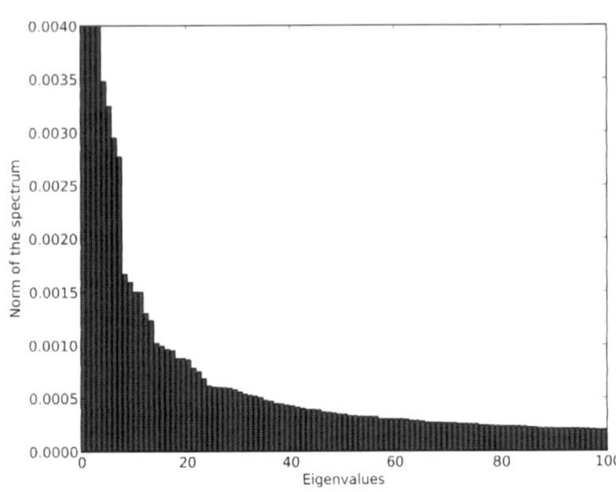


Figure 1: Eigenvalue distribution (limited to the first 100).

In order to "discover" the principles behind the co-occurrences, we examine eigenvectors associated with the largest eigenvalues. Some of the vectors indeed appear to have their interpretations or at least one could name common properties of involved words. The meaning of vectors becomes usually apparent after examination of the first few top component weights.

The list below consits of four eigenvectors, top three and the eighth one (as ordered according to their eigenvalues), along with five terms with highest absolute weights and interpretations of each vector.

1 *sztuczny* (artificial), *liryczny* (lyrical), *upiorny* (ghastly), *zrzędliwy* (grouchy), *przejrzysty* (lucid).
⇒ abstract properties one could attribute to an actor or a play.

2 *instynktowny* (instinctive), *odlotowo* (super/cool), *ostrożny* (careful), *bolesny* (painful), *przesadnie* (excessively)
⇒ physical and sensual experiences

3 *wyemancypować* (emancipate), *opuszczony* (abandoned), *przeszywać* (pierce), *wścibski* (inquisitive), *jednakowo* (alike)
⇒ unpleasant states and behaviours

8 *gładki* (smooth), *kochany* (beloved), *starać się* (make efforts), *niedołężny* (infirm), *intymnie* (intimately)
⇒ intimacy, caring, emotions

As it has been noted before, the eigenvectors of pure co-occurrence matrix $c$ did not deliver anything close in terms of conceivable interpretations. It is also fairly clear that some of the eigenvectors, as for example the third one, are more related to sentiment than the others. This is also evident by examination of average lexeme sentiment of top loaded terms of each vector, not disclosed in the paper.

The heuristic of SVD backed selection of paradigm words maximizes three factors:

- corpus frequency: avoid rare words where possible;
- eigenvector component weights: select words that contribute the most to a given eigenvector;
- sentiment polarity: select words with the highest absolute human scores.

## 8 Affinity Propagation

Affinity Propagation (Frey and Dueck, 2007) method was selected because of two distinct advantages for our task. First is the fact that it clusters data by diffusion in the similarity matrix, therefore does not require finding representations in Euclidean space. Second advantage, especially over cluster analysis algorithms such as k-means, is that the algorithm automatically sets its number of clusters and does not depend on initialization.

Affinity Propagation clusters data by exchanging real-valued messages between data points until a high-quality set of exemplars (representative examples, lexemes in our case) and corresponding clusters gradually emerges.

Interestingly, in each parameter setting the algorithm found exactly 156 clusters. It hints at the fact that the number of "latent" variables behind the co-occurrences could indeed be over 100. This is further confirmed by the percentage of norm of the spectrum covered by top 100 eigenvalues.

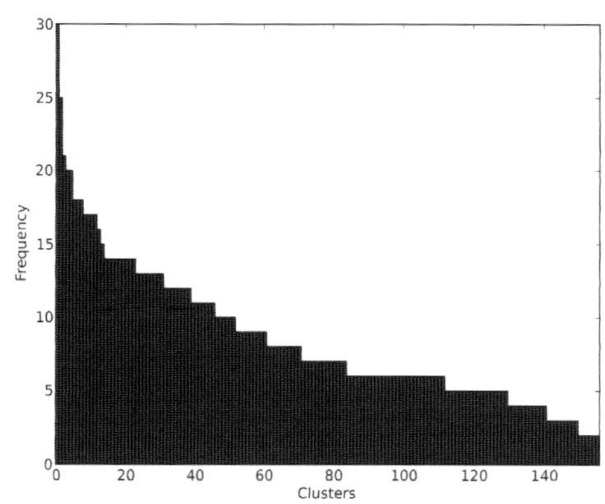


""

Figure 2: Histogram of cluster counts.

The five most frequent clusters cover only 116 words. We restrict the selection of paradigm words to the same frequency and polarity conditions as in the case of random method. We pick one paradigm word from each most frequent cluster because we assume that it is sufficient to approximate the principle which organizes that cluster. The heuristic is very similar to the one used in case of SVD.

## 9 Evaluation

Using continous SO-PMI and multi point scales for human scoring facilitates formulating the problem as a regression one, where goodness of fit of the estimations can be computed using different measures than in the case of classification.

This, however, demands a mapping such that ranges of the continuous SO-PMI scale correspond to discrete human scores. We propose to base such a mapping on dividing the SO-PMI range into 10 segments $\{s_0, ..., s_{10}\}$ of various length, each of which corresponds to one discrete human value.

The choice of values (locations) of specific points is a subject of minimization where the error function $E$ over a set of words $W$ is as follows:

$$E = \sum_{w \in W} dist(s_c, s_e)$$

For each word $w$, the distance function $dist$ returns the number of segments between the correct segment $s_c$ and the estimated segment $s_e$ using the SO-PMI. We minimize $E$ and find optimum locations for points separating each segment using Powell's conjugate direction method, determined the most effective for this task. Powell's algorithm is a non-gradient numerical optimization technique, applicable to a real valued function which does not need not be differentiable (Powell, 1964).

## 10 Results

Table 2 presents $E$ errors and extreme (min and max) SO-PMI values computed over two independent samples of 500 lexemes. Error columns indicated as $E$ denote errors computed either on non-optimized default ($def$) or optimized segments ($min$). Each combination of paradigm words and each sample required re-computing optimum values of points dividing the SO-PMI scale into segments.

Generally, the randomized selection method performs surprisingly well – most likely due to the fact that the frequency and polarity conditions are the key factors. In either case, the best result was obtained using the selection of paradigm words using the heuristic based on $svd$, closely followed by $aff$. In one case, random selection performed better than the $aff$.

| | | SO-PMI | | $E$ | |
|---|---|---|---|---|---|
| sample | | min | max | def | min |
| S1 | $r_1$ | -14 | 29 | 1226 | 908 |
| | $r_2$ | -15 | 23 | 1131 | 765 |
| | $r_3$ | -18 | 8.6 | 844 | 710 |
| | $aff$ | -9 | 25 | 1057 | 716 |
| | $svd$ | -13 | 26 | 1002 | 701 |
| S2 | $r_1$ | -18 | 19 | 983 | 812 |
| | $r_2$ | -17 | 15 | 910 | 756 |
| | $r_3$ | -11 | 20 | 1016 | 789 |
| | $aff$ | -13 | 28 | 1033 | 732 |
| | $svd$ | -13 | 35 | 1028 | 724 |

Table 2: SO-PMI ranges and error ($E$) values on two independent random samples of N=500. 3 randomized selections ($r_1 - r_3$), Affinity Propagation ($aff$) and SVD ($svd$).

The small margin of a victory could be explained by the fact that the size of each set of paradigm SO-PMI words is limited to five lexemes. Consequently, it is very difficult to represent a space of over one hundred latent variables – because such appears to be the number indicated by the distribution of eigenvalues in SVD and the number of clusters.

The ranges of SO-PMI values (in the columns min and max) were often non symmetric and leaned towards positive. This shift did not necessarily translate to higher error rates, especially after optimizations.

## 11 Discussion and Future Work

The methods presented in this article, based on the assumption of latent word co-occurrence structures, performed moderately better than the baseline of random selections. The result is ambiguous because it still requires a more in-depth understanding of underlying mechanims.

The work will be continued in several aspects. One is to pre-determine lexeme type before it is actually evaluated against particular members of paradigm word sets. This could be acheved using a two-step model consisting of lexeme type classification (with regard to over one hundred latent variables) followed by SO-PMI computation, where the selection of paradigm words is not fixed, as in this paper, but dependens on previously selected latent variables. Another promising direction is to focus on explanations and word features: how adding or removing particular words change the SO-PMI, and more importantly, why (in terms of features involved)? What are the features that change SO-PMI in specific directions? How to extract them?

## Acknowledgment

This research is supported by the POIG.01.01.02-14-013/09 project which is co-financed by the European Union under the European Regional Development Fund

## References

Brendan J. Frey and Delbert Dueck. 2007. Clustering by passing messages between data points. *Science*, 315:972–976.

Gregory Grefenstette, Yan Qu, David A. Evans, and James G. Shanahan, 2006. *Validating the Coverage of Lexical Resources for Affect Analysis and Automatically Classifying New Words along Semantic Axes*. Springer. Netherlands.

Roger A. Horn and Charles R. Johnson. 1990. *Matrix Analysis*. Cambridge University Press.

Animesh Mukherjee, Monojit Choudhury, and Ravi Kannan. 2009. Discovering global patterns in linguistic networks through spectral analysis: a case study of the consonant inventories. In *Proceedings of the 12th Conference of the European Chapter of the Association for Computational Linguistics*, EACL '09, pages 585–593, Stroudsburg, PA, USA. Association for Computational Linguistics.

Charles E. Osgood, George J. Suci, and Percy H. Tannenbaum. 1967. *The Measurement of Meaning*. University of Illinois Press.

M. J. D. Powell. 1964. An efficient method for finding the minimum of a function of several variables without calculating derivatives. *The Computer Journal*, 7(2):155–162, January.

Adam Przepiórkowski and Aleksander Buczyński. 2007.
spade: Shallow parsing and disambiguation engine. In *Proceedings of the 3rd Language & Technology Conference*, Poznań.

Adam Przepiórkowski, Rafał L. Górski, Barbara Lewandowska-Tomaszczyk, and Marek Łaziński. 2008. Towards the national corpus of polish. In *The proceedings of the 6th Language Resources and Evaluation Conference (LREC 2008), Marrakesh, Morocco*.

Adam Przepiórkowski, Mirosław Bańko, Rafał L. Górski, and Barbara Lewandowska-Tomaszczyk, editors. 2012. *Narodowy Korpus Języka Polskiego*. Wydawnictwo Naukowe PWN, Warsaw. Forthcoming.

J. Read and J. Carroll. 2009. Weakly supervised techniques for domain-independent sentiment classification. In *Proceedings of the 1st international CIKM workshop on Topic-sentiment analysis for mass opinion*, pages 45–52. ACM.

Robert Remus, Uwe Quasthoff, and Gerhard Heyer. 2006. Sentiws: a publicly available german-language resource for sentiment analysis. In *Proceedings of LREC*.

Peter Turney and Michael Littman. 2003. Measuring praise and criticism: Inference of semantic orientation from association. *ACM Transactions on Information Systems*, 21:315–346.

Peter D. Turney and Patrick Pantel. 2010. From frequency to meaning: vector space models of semantics. *J. Artif. Int. Res.*, 37:141–188, January.

Guangwei Wang and Kenji Araki. 2007. Modifying so-pmi for japanese weblog opinion mining by using a balancing factor and detecting neutral expressions. In *Human Language Technologies 2007: The Conference of the North American Chapter of the Association for Computational Linguistics; Companion Volume, Short Papers*, NAACL-Short '07, pages 189–192, Stroudsburg, PA, USA. Association for Computational Linguistics.

# Improving Machine Translation of Null Subjects in Italian and Spanish

**Lorenza Russo, Sharid Loáiciga, Asheesh Gulati**
Language Technology Laboratory (LATL)
Department of Linguistics – University of Geneva
2, rue de Candolle – CH-1211 Geneva 4 – Switzerland
{lorenza.russo, sharid.loaiciga, asheesh.gulati}@unige.ch

## Abstract

Null subjects are non overtly expressed subject pronouns found in *pro-drop* languages such as Italian and Spanish. In this study we quantify and compare the occurrence of this phenomenon in these two languages. Next, we evaluate null subjects' translation into French, a "non pro-drop" language. We use the Europarl corpus to evaluate two MT systems on their performance regarding null subject translation: Its-2, a rule-based system developed at LATL, and a statistical system built using the Moses toolkit. Then we add a rule-based preprocessor and a statistical post-editor to the Its-2 translation pipeline. A second evaluation of the improved Its-2 system shows an average increase of 15.46% in correct pro-drop translations for Italian-French and 12.80% for Spanish-French.

## 1 Introduction

Romance languages are characterized by some morphological and syntactical similarities. Italian and Spanish, the two languages we are interested in here, share the *null subject parameter*, also called the *pro-drop parameter*, among other characteristics. The null subject parameter refers to whether the subject of a sentence is overtly expressed or not (Haegeman, 1994). In other words, due to their rich morphology, Italian and Spanish allow non lexically-realized subject pronouns (also called null subjects, zero pronouns or pro-drop).[1]

From a monolingual point of view, regarding Spanish, previous work by Ferrández and Peral (2000) has shown that 46% of verbs in their test corpus had their subjects omitted. Continuation of this work by Rello and Ilisei (2009) has found that in a corpus of 2,606 sentences, there were 1,042 sentences without overtly expressed pronouns, which represents an average of 0.54 null subjects per sentence. As for Italian, many analyses are available from a descriptive and theoretical perspective (Rizzi, 1986; Cardinaletti, 1994, among others), but to the best of our knowledge, there are no corpus studies about the extent this phenomenon has.[2]

Moreover, althought null elements have been largely treated within the context of Anaphora Resolution (AR) (Mitkov, 2002; Le Nagard and Koehn, 2010), the problem of translating from and into a pro-drop language has only been dealt with indirectly within the specific context of MT, as Gojun (2010) points out.

We address three goals in this paper: i) to compare the occurrence of a same syntactic feature in Italian and Spanish, ii) to evaluate the translation of null subjects into French, that is, a "non pro-drop" language; and, iii) to improve the translation of null subjects in a rule-based MT system. Next sections follow the above scheme.

## 2 Null subjects in source corpora

We worked with the Europarl corpus (Koehn, 2005) in order to have a parallel comparative corpus for Italian and Spanish. From this corpus, we manually analyzed 1,000 sentences in both languages. From these 1,000 sentences (26,757 words for Italian, 27,971 words for Spanish), we identified 3,422 verbs for Italian and 3,184 for

[1] Henceforth, the terms will be used indiscriminately.

[2] Poesio et al. (2004) and Rodríguez et al. (2010), for instance, focused on anaphora and deixis.

Spanish. We then counted the occurrences of verbs with pro-drop and classified them in two categories: personal pro-drop[3] and impersonal pro-drop[4], obtaining a total amount of 1,041 pro-drop in Italian and 1,312 in Spanish. Table 1 shows the results in percentage terms.

| | Total Verbs | Pers. pro-drop | Impers. pro-drop | Total pro-drop |
|---|---|---|---|---|
| IT | 3,422 | 18.41% | 12.01% | 30.42% |
| ES | 3,182 | 23.33% | 17.84% | 41.17% |

Table 1: Results obtained in the detection of pro-drop.

Results show a higher rate of pro-drop in Spanish (10.75%). It has 4.92% more personal pro-drop and 5.83% more impersonal pro-drop than Italian. The contrast of personal pro-drop is due to a syntactic difference between the two languages. In Spanish, sentences like (1a.) make use of two pro-drop pronouns while the same syntactic structure uses a pro-drop pronoun and an infinitive clause in Italian (1b.), hence, the presence of more personal pro-drop in Spanish.

(1) a. **ES** $_{pro}$ le pido (1.sg) que $_{pro}$ intervenga (3.sg) con el prestigio de su cargo.
    b. **IT** $_{pro}$ le chiedo (1.sg) di intervenire (inf.) con il prestigio della sua carica.
    *I ask you to intervene with the prestige of your position.*

The difference of impersonal pro-drop, on the other hand, is due to the Spanish use of an impersonal construction (2a.) with the "*se*" particle. Spanish follows the schema "*se* + finite verb + non-finite verb"; Italian follows the schema "finite verb + *essere* (*to be*) + past participle" (2b.). We considered this construction formed by one more verb in Italian than in Spanish as shown in examples (2a.) and (2b.). This also explains the difference in the total amount of verbs (Table 1).

(2) a. ES Se podrá corregir.
    b. IT Potrà essere modificato.
    *It can be modified.*

[3]Finite verbs with genuinely referential subjects (i.e. *I, you, s/he, we, they*).

[4]Finite verbs with non-referential subjects (i.e. *it*).

We found a total number of non-expressed pronouns in our corpus comparable to those obtained by Rodríguez et al. (2010) on the Live Memories corpus for Italian and by Recasens and Martí (2010) on the Spanish AnCora-Co corpus (Table 2). Note that in both of these studies, they were interested in co-reference links, hence they did not annotate impersonal pronouns, claiming they are rare. On the other hand, we took all the pro-drop pronouns into account, including impersonal ones.

| Corpus | Language | Result |
|---|---|---|
| Our corpus | IT | 3.89% |
| Live Memories | IT | 4.5% |
| Our corpus | ES | 4.69% |
| AnCora-Co | ES | 6.36% |

Table 2: Null-subjects in our corpus compared to Live Memories and AnCora-Co corpora. Percentages are calculated with respect to the total number of words.

## 3 Baseline machine translation of null subjects

The 1,000 sentences of our corpus were translated from both languages into French (IT→FR; ES→FR) in order to assess if personal pro-drop and impersonal pro-drop were correctly identified and translated. We tested two systems: Its-2 (Wehrli et al., 2009), a rule-based MT system developed at the LATL; and a statistical system built using the Moses toolkit out of the box (Koehn et al., 2007). The latter was trained on 55,000 sentence pairs from the Europarl corpus and tuned on 2,000 additional sentence pairs, and includes a 3-gram language model.

Tables 3 and 4 show percentages of correct, incorrect and missing translations of personal and impersonal null subjects calculated on the basis of the number of personal and impersonal pro-drop found in the corpus.

We considered the translation correct when the null pronoun is translated by an overt pronoun with the correct gender, person and number features in French; otherwise, we considered it incorrect. Missing translation refers to cases where the null pronoun is not generated at all in the target language.

We chose these criteria because they allow us to evaluate the single phenomenon of null subject

| Its-2 | | | | |
|---|---|---|---|---|
| **Pair** | **Pro-drop** | **Correct** | **Incorrect** | **Missing** |
| IT→FR | personal | 66.34% | 3.49% | 30.15% |
| | impersonal | 16.78% | 18.97% | 64.23% |
| | *average* | *46.78%* | *9.6%* | *43.61%* |
| ES→FR | personal | 55.79% | 3.50% | 40.70% |
| | impersonal | 29.29% | 11.40% | 59.29% |
| | *average* | *44.28%* | *6.93%* | *48.78%* |

Table 3: Percentages of correct, incorrect and missing translation of zero-pronouns obtained by Its-2. Average is calculated on the basis of total pro-drop in corpus.

| Moses | | | | |
|---|---|---|---|---|
| **Pair** | **Pro-drop** | **Correct** | **Incorrect** | **Missing** |
| IT→FR | personal | 71.59% | 1.11% | 27.30% |
| | impersonal | 44.76% | 11.43% | 43.79% |
| | *average* | *61%* | *5.18%* | *33.81%* |
| ES→FR | personal | 72.64% | 2.02% | 25.34% |
| | impersonal | 54.56% | 2.45% | 42.98% |
| | *average* | *64.78%* | *2.21%* | *33%* |

Table 4: Percentages of correct, incorrect and missing translation of zero-pronouns obtained by Moses. Average is calculated on the basis of total pro-drop in corpus.

translation. BLEU and similar MT metrics compute scores over a text as a whole. For the same reason, human evaluation metrics based on adequacy and fluency were not suitable either (Koehn and Monz, 2006).

Moses generally outperforms Its-2 (Tables 3 and 4). Results for the two systems demonstrate that instances of personal pro-drop are better translated than impersonal pro-drop for the two languages. Since rates of missing pronouns translations are considerable, especially for Its-2, results also indicate that both systems have problems resolving non-expressed pronouns for their generation in French. A detailed description for each system follows.

### 3.1 Results – Its-2

Its-2 obtains better results for IT→FR personal pro-drop (66.34%) than for ES→FR (55.79%), but worse for impersonal pro-drop translation (16.78% and 29.29% respectively, Table 3).

For IT→FR translation in particular, Its-2 usually translates an Italian personal pro-drop with an overt pronoun of incorrect gender in French. In fact, it tends to translate a female personal pro-drop with a masculine overt pronoun. This problem is closely related with that of AR: as the system does not have any module for AR, it cannot detect the gender of the antecedent, rendering the correct translation infeasible.

The number of correct translation of impersonal pro-drop is very low for both pairs. ES→FR reached 29.29%, while IT→FR only 16.78% (Table 3). The reason for these percentages is a regular mistranslation or a missing translation. As for the mistranslation, in the case of Spanish, Its-2 translates the "*se*" pronoun in impersonal sentences by the French sequence *qui est-ce que* (*who*) (3). We attribute this behaviour to a lack of generation rules.

(3) ES Por consiguiente, mi grupo solicita que **se** suprima este punto del día.
FR Par conséquent, mon groupe sollicite qu'**on** supprime ce point de l'agenda.
**ITS-2** * Par conséquent, mon groupe sollicite **qui est-ce que** supprime ce point du jour.
*Therefore, my group ask to delete this point from the agenda.*

With respects to missing pronouns in the target language (Table 3), percentages are quite high in both translation pairs (43.61% and 48.78% average missing pronouns respectively), especially with impersonal pro-drop. Let us take the exemple of ES→FR translation (59.29% missing pronouns): Its-2 never generates the French expletive pronouns *"ce, c', ça"* (*it*) (4a.). For IT→FR translation (64.23% missing pronouns), it almost never generates the French pronoun *"il"* (*it*) for the impersonal 3rd person pro-drop pronoun in Italian (4b.).

However, if the system generates the pronoun, it is likely to be a first or a second person singular pronoun (*"je, tu"* – *I, you*) in French, increasing then the percentages of incorrectly translated impersonal pro-drop.

(4) a. ES No es pedir demasiado.
FR Ce n'est pas trop demander.
ITS-2 * Pas est demander trop.
*It is not too much to ask.*

b. IT È vero che [. . . ].
FR Il est vrai que [. . . ].
ITS-2 * Vrai que [. . . ].
*It is true that [. . . ].*

### 3.2 Results – Moses

Moses produces the highest percentage of correct translations for both personal and impersonal pro-drop, particularly in ES→FR (72.64% and 54.56% respectively, Table 4).

When translating personal pro-drop from Italian, sometimes the system generates infinitive forms instead of finite verbs (5).

(5) IT Naturalmente accettiamo questo emendamento.
FR Bien sûr, **nous** acceptons cet amendement.
MOSES Bien sûr accepter cet amendement.
*Of course, we accept this amendment.*

When translating impersonal pro-drop from Italian, it performs worse (44.76%) because it tends not to generate the expletive pronoun (6).

Furthermore, for both source languages, Moses translates the impersonal pro-drop usually corre-

(6) IT Vorrei, come mi è stato chiesto da alcuni colleghi, osservare un minuto di silenzio.
FR J'aimerais, comme **il** m'a été demandé par certains collègues, observer une minute de silence.
MOSES J'aimerais, comme m'a été demandé par certains collègues, observer une minute de silence.
*I would like, as some collegues asked me, to observe a minute of silence.*

sponding to French pronoun *"on"* as the first plural personal pronoun (*"nous"* – *we*) (7a. and 7b.).

(7) a. IT Io credo che si debba dare la precedenza alla sicurezza.
FR Je crois qu'**on** doit donner la priorité à la sécurité.
MOSES Je crois que **nous** devons donner la priorité à la sécurité.
*I think that priority should be given to the safety.*

b. ES Como han demostrado los eventos recientes, queda mucho por hacer sobre este tema.
FR Comme l'ont montré les événements récents, **on** a encore beaucoup à faire sur ce thème.
MOSES Comme l'ont montré les événements récents, **nous** avons encore beaucoup à faire sur ce thème.
*As it has been shown by recent events, there is much left to do on this subject.*

## 4 Its-2 improvements

On the basis of this first evaluation, we tried to improve Its-2 pronoun generation when translating from Italian and Spanish. Two new components were added to the translation pipeline: a rule-based preprocessor, and a statistical post-editor. This section presents them in detail, along with the resources they rely on.

### 4.1 Rule-based preprocessing

Preprocessing of input data is a very common task in natural language processing. Statistical systems often benefit from linguistic preprocessing to deal with rich morphology and long distance reordering issues (Sadat and Habash, 2006; Habash, 2007). In our case, the idea behind this first component is to help the translation process of a rule-based system by reducing the amount of zero pronouns in the source document[5], ensuring that subject pronouns get properly transferred to the target language.

In order to assess the effect of this approach, we implemented a rule-based preprocessor taking as input a document in Italian or Spanish and returning as output the same document with dropped subject pronouns restored. It relies on two resources: a list of personal and impersonal verbs, and a part-of-speech tagging of the source document. We first present these two resources before describing the approach in more detail.

#### List of personal and impersonal verbs

This list simply contains surface forms of verbs. For our experiment, these forms were extracted from a subset of the Europarl corpus, where pro-drop verbs were manually annotated as taking a personal pronoun or an impersonal pronoun. This limits the coverage, but ensures domain-specific verb usage.

#### Part-of-speech tagging of the source document

Its-2, being a transfer-based system, relies on a parser to construct the syntactic structure of the source language and, from there, it transfers the syntactic structure onto the target language. Its-2 uses Fips (Wehrli, 2007), a multilingual parser also developed at LATL. Apart from the projection of syntactic structures, Fips produces part-of-speech tagging.

#### Outline of the approach

These are the steps followed by the preprocessor:

1. Read a part-of-speech tagged sentence.

2. Whenever a verb with no subject is encountered, check if it is a personal verb or an impersonal verb.

3. If it is a personal verb, generate the appropriate pronoun before the verb (the masculine form is generated for the third person); if it is an impersonal verb, do not generate any pronoun.

4. Check the sentence for reordering according to syntactic rules of the target language (e.g. move the generated pronoun before a proclitic already preceding the verb).

An example of preprocessed sentences is given in Figure 1.

### 4.2 Statistical post-editing

Since the work of Simard et al. (2007a), statistical post-editing (SPE) has become a very popular technique in the domain of hybrid MT. The idea is to train a statistical phrase-based system in order to improve the output of a rule-based system. The statistical post-editing component is trained on a corpus comprising machine translated sentences on the source side (translations produced by the underlying rule-based system), and their corresponding reference translations on the target side. In a sense, SPE "translates" from imperfect target language to target language. Both quantitative and qualitative evaluations have shown that SPE can achieve significant improvements over the output of the underlying rule-based system (Simard et al., 2007b; Schwenk et al., 2009).

We decided to incorporate a post-editing component in order to assess if this approach can specifically address the issue of dropped subject pronouns. We first present the training corpus before describing the approach in more detail.

#### Training corpus

To train the translation model, we translated a subset of the Europarl corpus using Its-2. The translations were then aligned with corresponding reference translations, resulting in a parallel corpus for each language pair, composed of 976 sentences for IT→FR and 1,005 sentences for ES→FR. We opted for machine translations also on the target side, rather than human reference translations, in order to ascertain if a parallel corpus produced in such a way, with significantly lesser cost and time requirements, could be an effective alternative for specific natural language processing tasks.

[5]In Italian and Spanish, even if a native speaker would not use subject pronouns in a given sentence, the same sentence with overtly expressed subject pronouns is grammatical. There might be a pragmatic difference, as pronouns are used in these languages when emphasis or contrast is desired (Haegeman, 1994).

| | |
|---|---|
| Source in Italian | $_{pro}$ La ringrazio, onorevole Segni, $_{pro}$ lo farò volentieri. |
| Preprocessed | **Io** la ringrazio , onorevole Segni , **io** lo farò volentieri . |
| | *I thank you, Mr. Segni, I will do it willingly.* |
| Source in Spanish | Todo ello, de conformidad con los principios que $_{pro}$ siempre hemos apoyado. |
| Preprocessed | Todo ello, de conformidad con los principios que **nosotros** siempre hemos apoyado. |
| | *All this, according to the principles we have always supported.* |

Figure 1: Output of the preprocessor: the pronoun in the first sentence is generated before the proclitic *lo*, and the pronoun in the second sentence is generated before the adverb "*siempre*" (*always*).

We reused the language model trained for the Moses experiment of Section 3.

**Outline of the approach**

We trained the SPE component using the Moses toolkit out of the box. With this setup, the final translation in French of a source sentence in Italian or Spanish can be obtained in two simple steps:

1. Translate a sentence using Its-2.
2. Give the translated sentence as input to the SPE component; the output of the SPE component is the final translation.

An example of post-edited translations is given in Figure 2.

### 4.3 Combination of preprocessing and post-editing

The two components described in the previous sections can be used separately, or combined together as the first and last elements of the same translation pipeline. With respect to the generation of pronouns, error analysis showed that the setup producing the best translations was indeed the combination of preprocessing and post-editing, which was therefore used in the full post-evaluation described in the next section. The example in Figure 3 illustrates progressive improvements (with respect to the generation of pronouns) achieved by using preprocessing and post-editing over the baseline Its-2 translation.

## 5 Post-evaluation

After adding the two components, we manually re-evaluated the translations of the same 1,000 sentences. Table 5 show percentages of correct, incorrect and missing translation of null subjects in a comparative way: the first columns show percentages obtained by the baseline Its-2 system[6] while the second columns show percentages obtained by the improved system.

Results show higher percentages of correct pro-drop translation for both language pairs, with an average increase of 15.46% for IT→FR, and 12.80% for ES→FR. Specifically, percentages of personal pro-drop translation for both pairs increased almost the same rate: 13.18% for IT→FR; 13.34% for ES→FR. It was not the case for impersonal pro-drop, where rates of the first pair augmented (18.98%), while the latter decreased (12.11%).

We explain this behaviour to a particular difficulty encountered when translating from Spanish, a language that largely prefers subjunctive mood clauses to other structures such as infinitive clauses. The problem arises because subjunctive tenses have a less distinctive morphology, with the same conjugation for the first and third person singular (9).

(9) **ES** $_{pro}$ le pido (1.sg) que $_{pro}$ estudie (3.sg) un borrador de carta.
**FR** Je vous demande d'étudier un brouillon de lettre.
**ITS-2** *Je (1.sg) demande que j'étudie (1.sg) un brouillon de charte.
*I ask you to study a draft letter.*

As a consequence of the improvement of personal pro-drop, only incorrect impersonal pro-drop translations decreased (Table 5). Indeed, if we consider personal pro-drop translation, we think that by means of restoring the pronouns for finite verbs, we also amplified the issue of AR. For instance, Italian uses the third singular person

[6] These percentages have already been discussed in section 3 and, in particular, in Table 3.

| | |
|---|---|
| Its-2 translation | Vous invite à voter à faveur de l'amendement approuvé à l'unanimité [...]. |
| Post-edited | **Je** vous invite à voter en faveur de l'amendement approuvé à l' unanimité [...]. |
| | *I invite you to vote in favour of the amendment unanimously approved [...].* |
| Its-2 translation | **Je** madame Présidente, voudrais réclamer l'attention sur un cas [...]. |
| Post-edited | Madame la Présidente, **je** voudrais réclamer l'attention sur un cas [...]. |
| | *Madam President, I would like to draw the attention on a case [...].* |

Figure 2: Output of the post-editor: the pronoun in the first sentence is restored, and the pronoun in the second sentence is moved to the correct position.

| | |
|---|---|
| Source in Italian | $_{pro}$ E' la prima volta che $_{pro}$ intervengo in Plenaria e $_{pro}$ devo ammettere di essere molto emozionato [...]. |
| Preprocessed | E' la prima volta che **io** intervengo in Plenaria e **io** devo ammettere di essere molto emozionato [...]. |
| Baseline | Qu'est la première fois qu'intervient dans *Plenaria et admettre de m'est beaucoup émus [...]. |
| Translation | |
| -after preprocessing | Est la première fois que **j'**interviens dans *Plenaria et **j'**admettre d'est beaucoup émus [...]. |
| -with post-editing | Qu 'est la première fois qu' intervient en plénière ont et admettre de s 'est très émus [...]. |
| -using both | **C 'est** la première fois que **j'** interviens en plénière ont et **j 'admettre** d' est très émus [...]. |
| | *It is the first time that I speak in the Plenary session and I admit to being [...].* |

Figure 3: Comparison of translation outputs: preprocessing leads to a better analysis of the sentence by Fips, as suggested by the presence of the pronouns "*j'*" (*I*), absent in the baseline translation, and post-editing further restores successfully the missing impersonal pronoun "*C'*" (*It*), whereas post-editing without preprocessing has no effect on pronoun generation.

| | | **Baseline Its-2** | | | **Improved Its-2** | | |
|---|---|---|---|---|---|---|---|
| **Pair** | **Pro-drop** | **Correct** | **Incorrect** | **Missing** | **Correct** | **Incorrect** | **Missing** |
| IT→FR | personal | 66.34% | 3.49% | 30.15% | 79.52% | 5.87% | 14.60% |
| | impersonal | 16.78% | 18.97% | 64.23% | 35.76% | 13.13% | 51.09% |
| | *average* | *46.78%* | *9.6%* | *43.61%* | *62.24%* | *8.73%* | *29%* |
| ES→FR | personal | 55.79% | 3.50% | 40.70% | 69.13% | 7.81% | 23.04% |
| | impersonal | 29.29% | 11.40% | 59.29% | 41.40% | 8.07% | 50.52% |
| | *average* | *44.28%* | *6.93%* | *48.78%* | *57.08%* | *7.92%* | *34.98%* |

Table 5: Percentages of correct, incorrect and missing translation of zero-pronouns. Results obtained by improved Its-2. Average is calculated on the basis of total pro-drop in corpus.

("*lei*") as a form of polite treatment, while French uses the second plural person ("*vous*"); however, Its-2 translates a restored pronoun for a finite verb in the third singular person as a finite verb in the third singular person in French too (8).

Gender discrepancies are an AR issue as well. For IT→FR, the problem of a female personal pro-drop translated by a masculine overt pronoun in French still remains.

Finally, rates of missing pronouns also decreased. In this case, improvements are significant: we obtained a gain of 14.61% for the IT→FR pair and 13.8% for the ES→FR pair. Specifically, we obtained better improvements for personal pro-drop than for impersonal pro-drop. For the latter we think that rates decreased

(8) **IT** Signora Presidente, mi permetta di parlare.
**FR** Madame la Présidente, **permettez-moi** de parler.
**ITS-2** Madame la Présidente, **permet-moi** de parler.
*Madam President, let me speak.*

thanks only to the post-editing phase. Indeed, as both Italian and Spanish do not have any possible overt pronoun to be restored in the pre-processing phase, any improvement responds to changes made by the post-editor. On the other hand, improvements obtained for personal pro-drop translation confirm that the combination of the pre-processing and the post-editing together can be very advantageous, as already discussed in section 4.3.

## 6 Future work

As already mentioned, we have not found the solution to some problems yet.

First of all, we would like to include an AR module in our system. As it is a rule-base system, some problems as the subject pronoun mistranslation in subordinated sentences can be fixed by means of more specific rules and heuristics. Besides, an approach based on binding theory (Büring, 2005) could be effective as deep syntactic information is available, even though limited. For example, binding theory does not contain any formalization on gender, reason why a specific statistical component could be a more ideal option in order to tackle aspects such as masculine/feminine pronouns.

Secondly, an overt pronoun cannot be restored from a finite impersonal verb without making the sentence ungrammatical; therefore, our approach is not useful for treating impersonal sentences. As a consequence, we think that an annotation of the empty category, as done by Chung and Gildea (2010), could provide better results.

Also, in order to correctly render the meaning of a preprocessed sentence, we plan to mark restored subject pronouns in such a way that the information about their absence/presence in the original text is preserved as a feature in parsing and translation.

Finally, we would like to use a larger corpus to train the SPE component and compare the effects of utilizing machine translations on the target side versus human reference translations. Besides, we would like to further explore variations on the plain SPE technique, for example, by injecting Moses translation of sentences being translated into the phrase-table of the post-editor (Chen and Eisele, 2010).

## 7 Conclusion

In this paper we measured and compared the occurrence of one syntactic feature – the null subject parameter – in Italian and Spanish. We also evaluated its translation into a "non pro-drop" language, that is, French, obtaining better results for personal pro-drop than for impersonal pro-drop, for both Its-2 and Moses, the two MT systems we tested.

We then improved the rule-based system using a rule-based preprocessor to restore pro-drop as overt pronouns and a statistical post-editor to correct the translation. Results obtained from the second evaluation showed an improvement in the translation of both sorts of pronouns. In particular, the system now generates more pronouns in French than before, confirming the advantage of using a combination of preprocessing and post-editing with rule-based machine translation.

## Acknowledgments

This work has been supported in part by the Swiss National Science Foundation (grant No 100015-130634).

## References

Daniel Büring. 2005. *Binding Theory*. Cambridge Textbooks in Linguistics.

Anna Cardinaletti. 1994. Subject Position. *GenGenP*, 2(1):64–78.

Yu Chen and Andreas Eisele. 2010. Hierarchical Hybrid Translation between English and German. In *Proceedings of the 14th Annual Conference of the European Association for Machine Translation*, pages 90–97.

Tagyoung Chung and Daniel Gildea. 2010. Effects of Empty Categories on Machine Translation. In *Proceedings of the 2010 Conference on Empirical Methods in Natural Language Processing*, EMNLP '10, pages 636–645.

Antonio Ferrández and Jesús Peral. 2000. A Computational Approach to Zero-pronouns in Spanish. In *Proceedings of the 38th Annual Meeting of the*

*Association for Computational Linguistics*, pages 166–172.

Anita Gojun. 2010. Null Subjects in Statistical Machine Translation: A Case Study on Aligning English and Italian Verb Phrases with Pronominal subjects. Diplomarbeit, Institut für Maschinelle Sprachverarbeitung, University of Stuttgart.

Nizar Habash. 2007. Syntactic Preprocessing for Statistical Machine Translation. In *Proceedings of Machine Translation Summit XI*, pages 215–222.

Liliane Haegeman. 1994. *Introduction to Government and Binding Theory*. Blackwell Publishers.

Philipp Koehn and Christof Monz. 2006. Manual and Automatic Evaluation of Machine Translation between European Languages. In *Proceedings on the HTL-NAACL Workshop on Statistical Machine Translation*, pages 102–121. Association for Computational Linguistics.

Philipp Koehn, Hieu Hoang, Alexandra Birch, Chris Callison-Burch, Marcello Federico, Nicola Bertoli, Brooke Cowan, Wade Shen, Christine Moran, Richard Zens, Christopher J. Dyer, Ondřej Bojar, Alexandra Constantin, and Evan Herbst. 2007. Moses: Open Source Toolkit for Statistical Machine Translation. In *Proceedings of the 45th Annual Meeting of the Association for Computational Linguistics Companion Volume Proceedings of the Demo and Poster Sessions*, pages 177–180. Association for Computational Linguistics.

Philipp Koehn. 2005. Europarl: A Parallel Corpus for Statistical Machine Translation. In *Proceedings of the 10th Machine Translation Summit (MT Summit X)*.

Ronan Le Nagard and Philipp Koehn. 2010. Aiding Pronoun Translation with Co-Reference Resolution. In *Proceedings of the Joint 5th Workshop on Statistical Machine Translation*, pages 258–267.

Ruslan Mitkov. 2002. *Anaphora Resolution*. Longman.

Massimo Poesio, Rodolfo Delmonte, Antonella Bristot, Luminita Chiran, and Sara Ronelli. 2004. The VENEX corpus of anaphora and deixis in spoken and written Italian. In *Manuscript*.

Marta Recasens and M. Antònia Martí. 2010. AnCora-CO: Coreferentially Annotated Corpora for Spanish and Catalan. *Language Resources and Evaluation*, 44(4):315–345.

Luz Rello and Iustina Ilisei. 2009. A Rule-Based Approach to the Identification of Spanish Zero Pronouns. In *Proceedings of Student Research Workshop, RANLP*, pages 60–65.

Luigi Rizzi. 1986. Null Objects in Italian and the Theory of *pro*. *Linguistic Inquiry*, 17(3):501–557.

Kepa J. Rodríguez, Francesca Delogu, Yannick Versley, Egon W. Stemle, and Massimo Poesio. 2010. Anaphoric Annotation of Wikipedia and Blogs in the Live Memories Corpus. In *Proceedings of the Seventh International Conference on Language Resources and Evaluation (LREC)*, Valletta, Malta. European Language Resources Association (ELRA).

Fatiha Sadat and Nizar Habash. 2006. Combination of Arabic Preprocessing Schemes for Statistical Machine Translation. In *Proceedings of the 21st International Conference on Computational Linguistics and 44th Annual Meeting of the ACL*, pages 1–8.

Holger Schwenk, Sadaf Abdul-Rauf, Loïc Barrault, and Jean Senellart. 2009. SMT and SPE Machine Translation Systems for WMT'09. In *Proceedings of the 4th Workshop on Statistical Machine Translation*, pages 130–134.

Michel Simard, Cyril Goutte, and Pierre Isabelle. 2007a. Statistical Phrase-based Post-editing. In *Proceedings of NAACL HLT 2007*, pages 508–515.

Michel Simard, Nicola Ueffing, Pierre Isabelle, and Roland Kuhn. 2007b. Rule-based Translation With Statistical Phrase-based Post-editing. In *Proceedings of the 2nd Workshop on Statistical Machine Translation*, pages 203–206, June.

Eric Wehrli, Luka Nerima, and Yves Scherrer. 2009. Deep Linguistic Multilingual Translation and Bilingual Dictionaries. In *Proceedings of the Fourth Workshop on Statistical Machine Translation*, pages 90–94.

Eric Wehrli. 2007. Fips, a "Deep" Linguistic Multilingual Parser. In *Proceedings of the Workshop on Deep Linguistic Processing*, pages 120–127. Association for Computational Linguistics.

# Author Index

**Association for Computational Linguistics**
209 N. Eighth Street
Stroudsburg, Pennsylvania 18360

proceedings.com

# 60th Annual Meeting of the Association for Computational Linguistics (ACL 2022)

Tutorial Abstracts

Dublin, Ireland
22-27 May 2022